GLOBETR

TRAVEL GUIDE

BRITTANY

MAX WOOLDRIDGE

NEW
HOLLAND

GLOBETROTTER

TRAVEL GUIDE

First published in 1996 by New Holland
(Publishers) Ltd
London • Cape Town • Sydney • Singapore

Copyright © 1996 in text: Max Wooldridge
Copyright © 1996 in maps: Globetrotter Travel
Maps
Copyright © 1996 in photographs: Individual
photographers as credited
Copyright © 1996 New Holland (Publishers) Ltd

ISBN: 1 85368 422 8

New Holland (Publishers) Ltd
24 Nutford Place, London W1H 6DQ

Commissioning Editor: Tim Jollands
Project Manager: Elizabeth Frost
Editor: Brigitte Lee
Editorial Assistant: Justine Brown
Design: Philip Mann, ACE Ltd
Cartography: Globetrotter Travel Maps/ML
Design, London

Typeset by Philip Mann, ACE Ltd
Reproduced in Singapore by P&W Graphics
PTE Ltd
Printed and bound in Hong Kong by South
China Printing Company (1988) Limited

Although every effort has been made to ensure
accuracy of facts, and telephone and fax num-
bers in this book, the publishers will not be held
responsible for changes that occur at the time of
going to press.

Photographic credits: **Dorothy Burrows**, page 16;
French Picture Library, pages 68, 118, 119; **Brian
Harding**, page 39; **Roger Hilton**, page 69;
Andrew Land, pages 29, 75, 78, 81, 91; **Gordon
Lethbridge**, page 10; **Stuart Lumb**, page 24;
Photobank, front cover (top and bottom left),
pages 1, 4, 9, 19, 26, 28, 33, 38, 42, 52, 57, 58, 66,
67, 76, 77, 83 (bottom), 85, 87, 96, 99, 101, 104,
107, 109, 112, 113, 114, 115; **Norman Rout**, pages
59, 61, 65, 72; **Gino Russo**, pages 6, 8, 21, 79, 93;
Barrie Smith, page 62; **Jeroem Snijders**, title
page and pages 7, 12, 20, 22, 23, 37, 40, 55, 83
(top), 89; **Nigel Tisdall**, pages 11, 13, 14, 15,
17,18, 25, 27, 30, 35, 36, 41, 45, 46, 48, 63, 64, 88,
92, 102, 105, 110; **Linda Whitwam**, front cover
(top and bottom right)

The publishers and author wish to thank the following people for their assistance in this
project:

Elizabeth Powell and Marc Humphries at the
French Tourist Office in London; staff at the
Comité Régional de Tourisme in Brittany;
Andrew Barraclough at the Brittany Ferries
Information Bureau; Alain and Joelle Dolbeau in
St-Malo; Nicholas and Una Louarn in Locronan;
Marc and Anne Gauthier in Auray St Goustan;
Yann Le Gaudion, Annie ViGouroux and
Amanda McLean.

Front cover photographs
Top left: *Clifftop view of La Plage de la Mine d'Or at
Penestin.* **Top right**: *Ramparts of the medieval town
of Vannes.* **Bottom right**: *Brittany's ancient heritage
is evident in the Standing Stones at Carnac.* **Bottom
left**: *Fishermen gather nets at the picturesque
harbour of La Trinité.*

Title page photograph
*Dramatic coastal scenery of the Quiberon Peninsula
along the aptly named Côte Sauvage or Wild Coast of
Morbihan.*

CONTENTS

WATERSTONES BOOKSELLERS

1
Introducing Brittany

A lone body bent double on the beach at low tide, searching for mussels; colourful trawlers at anchor in harbours of pretty little ports; seabirds delicately balancing on rocks that look like they could tip at any moment; old ladies dressed in black, leaning close to one another to exchange gossip.

Everyone has his or her own favourite enduring image of Brittany – the popular holiday destination in the top left-hand Celtic corner of France. Shaped like a lobster's claw, geographically Brittany looks ready to crawl away from the rest of mainland France back towards its Celtic ancestors in Wales and Cornwall.

Brittany comprises four regions (*départements*) – **Ille-et-Vilaine**, **Côtes d'Armor**, **Finistère** and **Morbihan** – and the further west you go the more you'll hear French spoken with a distinctly Celtic accent.

Brittany is a relaxing place of simple pleasures. Its unspoilt charm in many places seems to have bypassed much of the 20th century. In picturesque towns and medieval villages such as **Dinan**, **Auray St-Goustan** and **Tréguier**, it feels as though nothing has changed since the Middle Ages. The imposing castles at **Vitré** and **Fougères** evoke scenes of battle with Normandy along Brittany's eastern frontier.

After his death, the warrior-knight and High Constable of France, Bertrand du Guesclin, left his heart in Brittany (actually, in the church of St-Sauveur in Dinan). Spiritually, it's likely that you'll leave a little of yours in Brittany, too.

TOP ATTRACTIONS

** **St-Malo**: the chic walled City of Corsaires
*** **Mont-St-Michel**: only a short drive from St-Malo
*** **Dinan**: an old fortress town with cobbled streets
** **Douarnenez**: charming port in the heart of Finistère
*** **Locronan**: picture-postcard town, in Finistère
*** **Quimper**: the longer you stay, the harder it is to leave this most Breton of cities
** **Belle-Ile**: an island off the Quiberon Peninsula that lives up to its name.

Opposite: *The busy port of Audierne in south Finistère.*

THE ARMORICAN MASSIF

As a result of tremendous upheaval in the earth's crust over 600 million years ago, high mountainous areas composed of granite and volcanic rock emerged through the waters that covered what is now France. In the course of time, the mighty peaks of the Armorican Massif became worn down into steep cliffs, rocky outcrops and gentle hills. Today, the highest points of the two plateaux that form the Armorican Massif – the Monts d'Arrée and the Montagnes Noires – do not exceed about 300m (1083ft).

THE LAND

Brittany's ancient name of Armorica ('land of the sea') is a reflection of the sea's historical importance in shaping the lives of the people who inhabit this region. Brittany's coast accounts for over a third of France's seaboard – 1200km (750 miles) of proud coastline consisting of dunes, rocky coves, cliffs and bays, where the natural elements of wind and sea rule the waves. Stretching from the **Côte d'Emeraude** (Emerald Coast) in the north and across the Channel coast of **Côtes d'Armor**, the coastline becomes more rugged around Finistère, with its many rocky promontories, until it reaches the southernmost Atlantic coast of Morbihan, where sandy beaches are perfect for bathing.

It was from this varied coastline that Bretons first set forth to earn their crust through fishing, exploration, shipping, piracy and smuggling. And Brittany's coasts continue to be lucrative, drawing millions of visitors to explore its myriad coastal attractions, from the sea-battered, wild coastlines of Finistère to the popular holiday resorts of the Côte d'Emeraude and the **Côte de Granit Rose** (Pink Granite Coast) in the north, and miles of soft, sandy beaches in the south.

Yet Brittany is also a region dominated by a people's affinity for stone – from the mysterious prehistoric megaliths at **Carnac** in the gentler climate of Morbihan on Brittany's south coast, to the stone-carved calvaries of the **Pays de Léon** in north Finistère – where the local people hold on to traditions and beliefs as strong as the granite that built their stone farmhouses.

Climate

In Brittany, even the most sensible holiday makers will have waterproofs with them

The rocky coastline of northwest Finistère at Cap de la Chèvre, jutting into Douarnenez Bay.

Perfect cycling country – Brittany's natural landscape lends itself to two-wheeled exploration. Distances are not great, hills are manageable, and the scenery is invariably delightful.

on sunny days. Bretons say that it rains every day in Brittany, and twice on Sundays. The region has a fairly settled climate year round, but the proximity of the sea means that there are frequent changes in weather. Visitors claim that it is not uncommon to experience all four seasons in one day. No wonder its fast-changing skies proved such a fascination for Paul Gauguin and his fellow artists of the Pont-Aven School.

Brittany has mild winters, with average temperatures ranging between 6°C (43°F) and 8°C (46°F), and warm summer temperatures averaging between 18°C (65°F) and 20°C (70°F). The sunnier southern coast of Morbihan has consistent warm temperatures between June and often as late as mid-October, but it can be wet and windy, especially along the coast of Finistère.

Flora and Fauna

In Brittany the hills are alive with the sound of wind blowing against all sorts of flora and fauna. It is not just woodland and heathland areas that offer a multitude of wildlife. Brittany has a rich and diverse hedgerow, so you might be advised to pack some binoculars.

Inland Brittany was once a heavily forested region, as indicated by its Celtic name, *Argoat*. However, commercial forestry and felling have contributed to the depletion of forest cover, and woods have largely given

PLACE NAMES

Major towns such as Rennes and Vannes are named after Gallic tribes (Redones, Veneti). However, when the Celts were driven out of Britain in the 5th century, many brought their place names with them. Brittany's often tongue-twisting names are made easier to understand by looking at the prefix, which can provide a clue as to the origins of a town:

Plou, **Pleu** or **Plo** (e.g. Ploërmel, Plougasnou) – a parish.

Ker (e.g. Kerzerho) – a house or village.

Lan or **Lam** (e.g. Landivisiau, Lamballe) – the church of, the holy place of.

Quim (e.g. Quimper, Quimperlé) – from the Breton *kemper*, a confluence of rivers.

Tré (e.g. Tréguier, Trébeurden) – a hamlet.

Loc (e.g. Loctudy, Locmariaquer) – a sacred place.

Gui (e.g. Guimiliau) – a town or borough.

ISLANDS OF BRITTANY

Too often neglected are Brittany's offshore islands:

Ile de Bréhat: tranquil island happily stuck in a pleasant time-warp just north of Paimpol.

Les Sept-Iles: seven islets make up Brittany's oldest nature reserve just north of the Côte de Granit Rose.

Ile de Batz: an island with a mild climate 15 minutes off the coast of Roscoff.

Ile d'Ouessant (Ushant): wild, windswept archipelago of eight islands off the Côte de Léon. Nearby, a dozen small islands make up the Molène archipelago.

Ile de Sein: just 8km (5 miles) from Finistère's westernmost tip, the dramatic Pointe du Raz.

Iles des Glénans: eight main islands with surrounding outcrops, home to a diversity of birdlife, off Finistère's southern coast.

Ile de Groix: a seabird reserve off the coast of Lorient.

Belle-Ile: the largest and most beautiful of Brittany's islands, with neighbouring islands of Houat and Hoëdic.

way to a more varied countryside. In the north and west, the landscape is predominantly agricultural, while central and eastern Brittany have extensive deciduous woods, notably the ancient **Forêt de Paimpont**, legendary home to King Arthur.

Hedgerows seem to make up for the lack of forests, and there is a wealth of colourful flora on display, including primroses, buttercups, orchids and red campion. If there's a bustle in the hedgerow, don't be alarmed – it's more than likely going to be any number of birds, including blackbirds, starlings, bullfinches, great tits, chiff-chaffs, robins and magpies. The ground is the domain of the brown hare, mole, hedgehog and vole. In woodland areas, badgers, foxes and bank voles roam.

Brittany's heathland is dominated by bright yellow gorse, which is in flower all year round and can reach a height of 2m (6ft). Broom, purple heather and cross-leaved heath also grow in profusion on cliffs and hilltops. Birds that make their nests in Brittany's heathland include the Dartford warbler, yellowhammer, kestrel, linnet and greenfinch.

You won't go far in Brittany without seeing hydrangea growing in someone's garden, or geraniums creating a bright window display. Swallows, swifts, collared turtle-doves, house sparrows, barn owls and bats can all be found in inhabited areas.

Flecks of purple and yellow brighten the clifftop of Pointe du Raz, Brittany's westernmost headland. Heather, broom and gorse grow in abundance, providing a welcome splash of colour amid the dour, grey-hued granite.

Brittany has two regional nature parks – the **Parc Naturel Régional d'Armorique** (Armorica Regional Nature Park) and the **Parc Naturel Régional de la Grande Brière** – which are both inhabited rural areas that strike a balance between economic development and preservation of natural, cultural and human resources.

Much of Finistère's most spectacular scenery lies within the boundaries of the Armorica Regional Nature Park, from the crags and heathland of the Monts d'Arrée to the wild and mysterious Ile d'Ouessant, stretching from the Crozon Peninsula to Huelgoat, over an expanse of Breton landscape that includes forests, moorland, valleys and coastline. Cycling and walking tours are an excellent way to see the park and to take in a number of the ornithological reserves in the area, with their populations of gannets and puffins as well as the marine life that it supports.

By way of a contrast from the beach at La Baule, just inland from St-Nazaire, the Grande Brière Nature Park covers 399km² (154 sq miles) of salt marshes and sites. The ecological wealth of this area led to its establishment in 1970 as a Regional Nature Park. There are many routes specifically designed for walking, cycling and horse-riding, and trips by punt through the reedbeds may yield sightings of otters.

Birdwatchers are in for a treat in Brittany. A number of reserves and protected sites along the coast offer ample opportunities to watch seabirds such as puffins, gannets, guillemots, razorbills, kittiwakes, shags, fulmars and oystercatchers, while inland, on the bracken-covered hills of the Monts d'Arrée in the Armorica Regional Nature Park, buzzard, hen harrier and stonechat can be spotted.

There are plenty of opportunities for watersports enthusiasts at Port Haliguen, Quiberon's easternmost port. Morbihan's more settled climate and fine sandy beaches also make for excellent family holidays.

NATURE PARK INFORMATION

For more information on the Parc Naturel Régional d'Armorique, contact Ménez-Meur, Hanvec, 29460 Daoulas, tel: 98.21.90.69; for information on the Parc Naturel Régional de la Grande Brière, contact 180, Ile de Fédrun, 44720 St-Joachim, tel: 40.88.42.72.

A burial chamber at Perros-Guirec, Côtes d'Armor. Evidence of prehistoric Brittany is visible throughout the peninsula, though very little is known about the region's inhabitants before the Roman conquest. Myths and legends abound.

HISTORY IN BRIEF

The first known signs of life in Brittany were recorded in 8000BC, and its earliest inhabitants were unknown tribes of hunter–gatherers responsible for the menhirs (standing stones) that are a feature of the landscape.

The first Celts arrived in Armorica in the 3rd and 4th centuries BC. By the 2nd century BC, the region was shared among five Gallic tribes, amongst them the Namnetes, Redones and Veneti, who lived roughly in the regions of what were to become the cities of Nantes, Rennes and Vannes.

Roman Occupation

Caesar started the Gallic wars in 58BC and, despite fierce maritime opposition from the Veneti, the Romans eventually proved victorious. Barbarian invasions encroached upon the Gallo-Roman empire in the 3rd century AD and weakened Roman domination; meanwhile, Vikings were attacking the coasts of Armorica. The Roman occupation lasted for four centuries before collapsing in the 4th century AD.

The Arrival of the Britons

The withdrawal of Roman troops following the collapse of Roman dominion had left both Britain and Gaul open to increased attacks by the Vikings from across the North

ANCIENT REMAINS

Although the lost city of Ys in Douarnenez Bay is the stuff of legend, there is proof that two places actually did disappear under water. A Gallo-Roman house found near the Ile de Sein and the Cromlech d'Er Lanic in the heart of the Golfe de Morbihan both vanished under the waves between 2000 and 3000 years ago.

HISTORICAL CALENDAR

8000BC First recorded signs of habitation in Brittany.

2nd century BC The region of Armorica is shared between five Gallic tribes, including the Namnetes, Redones and Veneti.

56BC Julius Caesar defeats his last Gallic enemies, the Veneti, in sea-battle and secures control over the entire region.

4th century AD Roman occupation comes to an end.

5th and 6th centuries Arrival of Celtic migrants fleeing Viking invasions into Britain. They give Brittany its new name, Petite Bretagne, later Bretagne, and found the first Christian churches.

799 Charlemagne unites the region under Frankish rule.

845 Nominoë appoints himself first Duke of Brittany.

851 Boundaries of Brittany firmly established by the time of Nominoë's death.

911 Norse chieftain Rollo becomes Duke of Normandy.

Normans subsequently invade Breton territory.

939 Normans expelled by Alain Barbe-Torte, who rules Brittany as king until his death in 952.

1364 Defeat of Charles de Blois by Jean de Montfort at Auray settles War of Succession for the duchy of Brittany.

1399–1442 Duke Jean V, the Wise, rules over a prospering and independent Brittany.

1488 Duke François II, father of Duchess Anne, defeated by Charles VIII of France at St-Aubin-du-Cormier.

1491 Anne agrees to marry Charles, but safeguards Brittany's independence.

1532 Treaty of Union with France formally ratified. End of Breton autonomy.

1534 St-Malo-born explorer, Jacques Cartier, adds Canada to France's colonial possessions.

1598 Edict of Nantes signed by Henri IV ends Wars of Religion

between Catholics and Protestants.

1675 'Stamped Paper' peasant revolts throughout Brittany against additional taxation imposed by Louis XIV.

1789 French Revolution breaks up Brittany. Counter-revolutionary rebellions led by Chouans following the introduction of conscription.

1804 Execution of Chouan leader, Georges Cadoudal.

19th century Fishing expeditions to Iceland and Newfoundland leave from the port of Paimpol.

1932 Breton nationalists blow up a statue in Rennes on 400th anniversary of Brittany's union with France.

1940 Every man of fighting age on the Ile de Sein responds to General de Gaulle's appeal to arms.

1962 Administrative reorganization places ancient Breton capital Nantes outside Brittany.

Sea. The incursion into Britain of Angles and Saxons in the 5th and 6th centuries drove one part of the indigenous population to retreat westwards; others headed across the water to Armorica. In order to distinguish their new homeland from the land they had left, Grande (Greater) Bretagne, Armorica was given the new name of Petite (Lesser) Bretagne, later Bretagne.

The new arrivals brought with them a Celtic language that their predecessors, under Roman rule, had ceased to use. Also part of their cultural baggage was the Christian religion, and they wasted no time in building their first churches. The names of many of these first Christian missionaries are preserved in the names of towns and villages along the Channel coast: St-Jacut-de-la-Mer, St-Cast-le-Guildo, St-Brieuc (from St Brioc), St-Pol-de-Léon (St Paul the Aurelian), St-Malo.

Parish close statuary carved in local granite has a naive yet powerfully expressive quality.

The ominous mass of Vitré's imposing château dominates the town. Built on a ridge overlooking the Vilaine river valley, the fortified castle was besieged by the English during the Hundred Years' War.

The five Armorican tribes were soon overwhelmed by two major clans, the Dumnonii, from Devon, who occupied the land in the north, and the Cornovii, from Cornwall, from whom the area of Cornouaille in the south derives its name. The next century saw the region as a whole divided between these two groupings, and it was only with the arrival of Charlemagne in 799 that Brittany was united, albeit under Frankish control.

Independence for Brittany

Disputes between Celts and Frankish peoples, which had begun in 751, resulted in the third son of Charlemagne – Louis the Pious – appointing the Breton nobleman Nominoë to keep the peace in the region. But five years after Louis' death in 840, Nominoë claimed independence for Brittany after defeating Louis' son Charles the Bald in battle at Redon. Nominoë crowned himself Brittany's first duke, and set about seizing Nantes and Rennes. By the time of his death in 851, the boundaries of Brittany had been firmly established.

The Norman Threat

With the decline of Frankish authority in the 9th century, Viking raids increasingly threatened Breton territory. In 911, the king of France, Charles the Simple, finally caved in to the Norse invaders and granted the title to the duchy of Normandy, on Brittany's eastern flank, to the

Viking chieftain, Rollo, in order to secure peace for his own people. The consequences for Brittany were, temporarily at least, disastrous.

In 919 the ever-present threat of incursion from its neighbour became reality when the Normans ran amok in Brittany. Most Breton leaders had fled to England and the Normans held sway until the son of a Breton nobleman, Alain Barbe-Torte, returned to lead victorious battles against the Normans in 939. Alain Barbe-Torte ruled as king until his death in 952, when Brittany reverted to being a duchy. While Brittany was determined to remain independent of France, sheer geography determined that, sooner or later, a union was inevitable.

Jean V succeeded Jean de Montfort as Duke of Brittany in 1399. His skilful administration of the region during a time of great upheaval earned him the nickname 'the Wise'. Here he is commemorated in a plaque at Dinard.

War and Peace

The War of Succession in 1341 for the duchy of Brittany was fought between Jean de Montfort and Charles de Blois, both relatives of Duke Jean III, who had died without heir. De Montfort won the support of the English King Edward III, and the two contenders met in bloody civil battles, aggravated by the Hundred Years' War, which had been simmering between England and France since 1337.

Charles de Blois was eventually defeated at the Battle of Auray in 1364, despite the presence in his army of one of France's greatest military heroes, Bertrand du Guesclin (see page 14). The following year, the French King Charles V recognized de Montfort as Jean IV of Brittany, and the ensuing period of the Montfort Dukes was one of the most golden in Breton history.

Breton involvement in the Hundred Years' War was minimized as a result of the neutral position adopted by Jean IV's successor, Duke Jean V, also known as the

THE BATTLE OF AURAY

It was against Bertrand du Guesclin's advice that Charles de Blois launched an attack at Auray on his cousin Jean de Montfort and his English allies. Charles' troops were badly positioned on a marshy plain north of the town, and military disaster was inevitable. Despite the death of Charles, du Guesclin continued to fight bravely, his courage on the battlefield earning him the praise of the English commander.

Bertrand du Guesclin (pronounced 'du Gecklan'), Breton warrior and later High Constable, spent his military career fighting against the English to drive them out of France – ironic, then, that the public gardens next to the church in Dinan where his heart is kept should be called the *English* gardens. Quite how he would feel about that no one knows.

Du Guesclin was born in 1320 at La Motte-Broons castle near Dinan, and later married a local draper's daughter named Typhaine. By 1370 he had achieved such high renown for his bravery in battle that he was promoted to High Constable of France, in effect commander-in-chief. He died in 1380 – naturally fighting the English – at Châteauneuf-de-Randon, in the Massif Central. His death brought France fighting for his remains – his body went to St-Denis in Paris, but he left his heart in Dinan's St-Sauveur church.

The greatest Breton hero of them all? Perhaps not. Du Guesclin is seen by many Bretons as a traitor for deeming the monarchy more important than his homeland when in 1373 he marched against Duke Jean IV of Brittany. In fact, in 1946, Breton nationalists were so disenchanted with the heroic status accorded to du Guesclin that they blew up his monument in the Thabor gardens in Rennes.

Wise, who presided over an increasingly prosperous economy from 1399 until his death in 1442. Jean's successors also managed to retain a degree of independence, although Brittany's strategic position, together with its earlier support for England, inevitably made it dangerous in the eyes of France, which came to the conclusion that the threat could only be subdued by Brittany's incorporation into its kingdom.

Union with France

Before his death in 1488, Duke François of Brittany had been compelled to sign a treaty with France following the Breton army's defeat at the hands of royalist troops in the battle of St-Aubin-du-Cormier. Under the terms of the treaty, François' daughter, the 11-year-old Anne, could marry only with France's consent.

Anne acceded to the duchy of Brittany on her father's death, marrying by proxy into the Hapsburg empire. Her betrothed, Maximilian of Austria, was a formidable soldier and heir to the Holy Roman Empire; the alliance naturally exacerbated France's fear of an independent Brittany and also contravened the terms of the treaty. The French king, Charles VIII, who was in theory betrothed to Maximilian's daughter, saw his opportunity and promptly marched his army into Brittany, capturing several key towns. Trapped by French troops in Rennes, Anne finally agreed to marry

Charles in 1491 in preference to watching her people endure further hardship.

Anne's marriage to Charles inevitably brought Brittany closer to France, although the duchy's independence was safeguarded by a shrewd marriage settlement. When Anne died in 1514, the duchy was bequeathed to Anne's daughter, Claude, who had married the future king of France, François I. The king's intention to incorporate his wife's lands into the French kingdom was realized in August 1532, when the Treaty of Union was formally ratified by the Breton parliament in Vannes, placing Brittany under the control of France. Henceforward, Brittany was to be administered by the central French system of government, although it was allowed to keep its own parliament in Rennes.

Union with France was not without benefit for Brittany. Breton architecture flourished, and many châteaux and churches were constructed at this time. Brittany also developed important trading links with the Americas, India and the Middle East, while the Breton explorer Jacques Cartier sailed from his home town of St-Malo in 1534, and added the newly discovered Canada to France's territorial possessions.

The Wars of Religion

Serious religious differences between Catholics and Protestants (Huguenots) fanned fresh conflict that turned into full-scale war. In 1588, Brittany's Catholic governor, the Duc de Mercoeur, revolted, proclaimed himself head of the Holy Catholic League and attempted to take over Brittany. Civil war erupted and Bretons asked Henri IV for help in restoring order. He responded by signing the Edict of Nantes in 1598, which promised religious freedom

ANNE DE BRETAGNE

For much of her life Duchess Anne of Brittany campaigned hard for Breton autonomy. Today she is held in esteem throughout the region for her devout faith as well as for battling for Brittany's right to support itself. Others, however, accuse her ultimately of selling out to the French.

Opposite: *The impenetrable stronghold of Fort la Latte.*

Below: *19th-century painting of a* pardon *arriving at Concarneau.*

THE CHOUANS

The Breton revolutionaries, known as the Chouans, were originally peasants-turned-guerrillas. They initially revolted against taxes levied to subsidize the French wars that followed the Vendée's first uprising when obligatory conscription was introduced by the new Republic in March 1793. The Chouans take their unusual name from Jean Cotterau and his band of insurgents from Maine: their private signal imitated the *chat-huant* call of the brown owl. There were three separate Chouan uprisings during the 1790s until 1800, when Napoleon dispensed with conscription and restored religious freedom on condition that the Chouans gave themselves up.

and tolerance for all. However, this new-found freedom did not apply for African slaves, who were being shipped to Brittany as part of a triangular trade in rum, sugar, spices and slaves – on the proceeds of which Nantes grew very fat indeed.

From Rebellions to Revolution

Intermittent peasant revolts against the injustices of rural nobility were a feature of the 17th century in France. Breton peasants revolted in 1675 when a law imposing additional taxation on tobacco and all legal documents was introduced by Louis XIV's finance minister, Jean-Baptiste Colbert. The 'Stamped Paper' revolts erupted in Rennes and Nantes before extending to the countryside, but all were brutally put down by royalist troops.

There were many infringements on Breton liberties during the reign of Louis XIV, and a series of burdensome taxes was imposed into the 18th century. No one was happier with the outbreak of the French Revolution in 1789 than the Bretons; to many it signalled the death knell for royalty. The first victims of the Revolution were killed during anti-aristocratic riots in Rennes in January 1789. But Breton fervour soon subsided when, less than six months later, Brittany had been wiped off the map, replaced by five *départements* dictated by Paris. Obligatory conscription provoked counter-revolutionary clashes by the Chouans, under

Detail from a piece of Quimper faïence. Typical designs show characters and scenes from Breton life and legend.

their leader Georges Cadoudal. He was later executed in 1804 after his plan to kidnap Napoleon failed, thereby bringing the rebellion to an end. In the following years Napoleon's ideas for centralization included numerous attempts to destroy the Breton language, and Bretons continued to be the butt of French jokes.

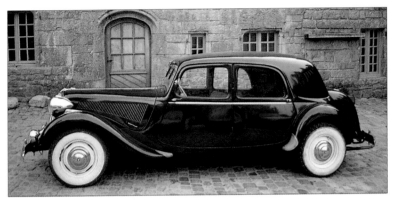

The 20th Century

The Great War of 1914–18 was a tragic time in Breton history, with the blood sacrifice of hundreds of thousands of Breton soldiers. Instead of receiving thanks, the Bretons and their culture continued to suffer when a law banning the language was eventually passed. This caused the first rumblings of an independence movement, and it wasn't long before a political movement began to emerge. Prominent among the militant nationalist groups was a secret society, Gwenn Ha Du, which took its name from the colours of the Breton flag, white and black.

During World War II Brittany saw plenty of military action and the entire region was occupied by German troops. Some Bretons openly collaborated with the Nazis, including some of the separatist groups. Others rejected the German claim that they were liberators freeing the Bretons from the tyranny of French occupation, and played an important part in the French Resistance. In June 1940 hundreds of young men rallied to General de Gaulle's call to arms – notably on the Ile de Sein, just off the coast of Finistère, where every man of fighting age volunteered to fight.

Isolated towns were badly damaged in heavy fighting, but coastal areas bore the brunt. Brittany's ports were important strategic points for Hitler and many of these were destroyed during the liberation by General

Medieval meets modern: a 20th-century classic car seems perfectly in keeping with its ancient setting in place de l'Eglise, Locronan. This charming town in the south of Finistère has been called the most picturesque in Brittany.

WARRING FACTIONS

World War II split the hearts and minds of the Bretons. Hundreds responded to General de Gaulle's call to arms and many Bretons joined the Allied forces in the North African and French campaigns. Others were involved in underground resistance movements like the *maquis*. Still others saw the Nazi occupation as a chance to attain Breton nationalist goals, and collaborated openly with the Nazis.

EXPLAINING THE BRETON FLAG

The two colours of the
traditional black and white
Breton flag (called the
Gwenn Ha Du) represent the
division of Brittany into two
linguistic regions, the Gallic
and the Breton. The flag
consists of a box of 11
ermines in the top left-hand
corner evoking the Duchy of
Brittany, and nine alternating
black and white stripes.
While the four white stripes
signify the Breton regions of
Léon, Cornouaille, Trégor and
Vannetais, the five black
stripes traditionally represent
the Gallic regions of Rennes,
Nantes, Dolois, Malouin and
Penthièvre.

Patton's Allied bombardments. After the war those
responsible for reconstruction were far kinder to the
former pirate stronghold of St-Malo than they were to
Lorient, Brest or St-Nazaire.

In the post-war period, Brittany emerged from its
isolation; traditional farming methods gave way to
modern agricultural techniques, and farming developed
into a giant operative industry. Brittany also realized its
potential for tourism and began to woo visitors to its
coastlines. Decentralization policies encouraged the
relocation of important industries to Brittany, including
the giant Citroën factory, which moved to Rennes.

Bretons now enjoy greater self-worth than ever
before; their language is no longer banned and folk
festivals and traditions are commonplace.

As a region of France, Brittany now faces whatever
problems France faces – from growing unemployment to
whether its local football clubs are trailing in the French
league. And yet, despite over four centuries of union,
Brittany has emerged with its distinct Celtic culture and
strong personality relatively unscathed.

Breton Nationalism

You can still see graffiti denouncing central rule from
Paris and 'Free the Bretons' posters in Celtic bars. To
these Breton nationalists, Brittany was and still is a
separate country, quite distinct from its Gallic neighbour.

Opposite: *Women don
traditional costume,
including white lace
coiffes, for a local* pardon
*at La Lorette, near
Quimper.*

Right: *Flying the flag. The
black and white Gwenn Ha
Du* (right), *designed by
Morvan Marchal in 1925,
is now raised proudly
alongside the French
tricolore at Dinard. Not so
long ago, any manifestation
of Breton nationalism was
harshly penalized.*

The traditional Breton culture and language, now widely seen at festivals and *pardons*, were once severely repressed. There was a time when schoolchildren caught speaking the Breton language were forced to lick the floor as punishment. And signs in public places read: 'No spitting or speaking Breton'.

At the end of the 19th century, a growing feeling of Breton nationalism had resulted in the formation of cultural and political associations. Some Bretons have been more desperate than others to keep their individuality, and attack rule from Paris, an authority that Breton writer Morvan Lebèsque contemptuously termed the 'garrison state'.

In 1932, Breton nationalists marked the 400th anniversary of Brittany's union with France by blowing up a statue in Rennes in which Brittany swears its allegiance to Louis XV. Later, in the 1960s and 1970s, there were sporadic outbursts of separatist violence, with the formation of the Breton Liberation Front, and small groups of extremists stoned police stations and carried out small-scale bombings.

Traditionally, when political power is lacking, cultural identity exists on a folklore level, and Brittany is no exception. Campaigns for Breton separatism have now died down, and the Bretons' independent character is largely preserved in the celebration of festivals, folklore and processions, and in the teaching of Celtic language and literature at universities. A number of Celtic Clubs have also sprung up to promote Breton music and culture.

Now, most Bretons accept that Brittany is a region of France and that their dreams of an independent nation have suffered a similar fate to that of the legendary drowned city of Ys, which lies submerged in Douarnenez Bay in Finistère.

PARDONS

Undoubtedly the most crystallized form of Breton culture and tradition is its numerous *pardons* – annual processions (usually in the summer) held in honour of a local saint and attended by locals and people from nearby villages, who pray for redemption for their sins. They follow a similar pattern; a solemn procession with banners and crosses is usually followed by much dancing and traditional Breton music and celebration. Watch out for the cider at these events, as it can be very potent.

GOVERNMENT AND ECONOMY

Industry

The sea still supplies Brittany with its three main sources of economic resources – commerce, fishing and tourism.

Fishing, traditionally one of Brittany's most important activities, is still heavily ingrained in the region's culture. Since the 1930s an increasing number of large factory ships have sailed to every corner of the globe, bringing back vast catches. But all over Brittany there are still small, high-quality in-shore fishing fleets that go out and back every day, bringing fresh fish back to harbour. However, in recent years cut-price imports have put many Breton fishermen out of work.

The natural Breton coastline, with its contrast of smooth, flat beaches regularly cleansed by the tide and wild rocky inlets, together with its high annual sunshine average, continues to make Brittany one of the most popular tourist destinations in France. A latecomer to industrialization, Brittany has not disfigured its countryside with ugly factories – at least, not yet.

Agriculture

Brittany's gardens may look pretty, but there are business brains responsible for the beauty. Traditional farming methods yielded to new systems that replaced

wheat with vegetables, and the region is now the premier French region for cereal and milk production, food processing and stock breeding.

Several of the small farms have given way to co-operatives, and small-scale farming has gradually developed into an industry. But many small, family-run farms still dot the landscape.

THE PEOPLE
The Breton Soul

Bretons can seem as mysterious as the *alignements* of prehistoric megalith stones at Carnac. Though by nature warm and generous, they are renowned for being hard to get to know, a reputation that they're not about to relinquish.

A seafaring, god-fearing race of fishermen and storytellers originally from Wales and Cornwall, Bretons are a melancholy people given to bouts of merriment rather than the other way round.

Above: *Collecting seaweed near Roscoff.*

The Breton soul is inherently sad, but not without humour – far from it. It's worth remembering that history has ingrained hardship and harsh living conditions into Breton culture, whether it is working the land or a sailor's life. Long sea voyages at the end of the 18th century would last a year or more, and it was normal for a third of the crew to die during the journey.

The French military traditionally used Breton soldiers as cannon fodder, and it was young Breton conscripts who would be the first to be sent to their deaths in the front line, especially in the bloody battles of World War I.

Bretons are a hard-working, reliable people who are true to their word. They have no problem expressing themselves as often and as loudly as possible. They are also a helpful and kind-hearted people – and if you're in any kind of trouble, they will certainly not hesitate in coming to your aid.

Bretons are traditionally conservative and yet restless; home-lovers who always ventured around the world in search of their fortune. Countless explorers, traders, missionaries and fishermen have set sail from the ports of Brest, St-Malo, Lorient and Nantes. It is this contradiction at the heart of their soul that gives Bretons their real spirit.

Opposite: *Brittany is one of France's prime agricultural regions.*

SOME BASIC FRENCH
Yes/no **Oui/non**
Please **S'il vous plaît**
Excuse me **Excusez-moi**
Thank you (very much) **Merci (beaucoup)**
Where is . . . ? **Où est . . . ?**
How much is it? **Combien est-ce?/C'est combien?**
Please help me **Aidez-moi, s'il vous plaît**
What time is it? **Quelle heure est-il?**
I don't understand **Je ne comprends pas**
Where are the toilets? **Où sont les toilettes?**
When does . . . open/close? **À quelle heure ouvre/ ferme . . . ?**

Opposite: *The Bigoudène coiffe is the tallest of all the Breton headdresses.*

Below: *The calvary at Guimiliau contains over 200 figures.*

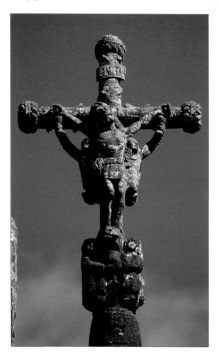

Language

Breton is not a dialect but a language. And a dying one, some will tell you. Traditionally, it is an ancient, melancholic tongue dealing in tales of love, witchcraft and sobering stories of sons away at sea. A Celtic language, it is closely related to Welsh and Cornish, and all three are mutually intelligible.

The increasing French influence and former suppression of the language has led to a decline in its usage, but since the 1970s the language is being taught again. Breton is traditionally spoken in Basse Bretagne (Lower Brittany), which encompasses the districts of Tréguier, Léon, Cornouaille and Vannes. You might hear it spoken on market days in towns in the Pays de Léon or in cathedrals such as Quimper in Finistère, where services are still sometimes conducted in Breton.

Religion

Bretons are a deeply religious people, predominantly Roman Catholic, whose beliefs have weathered as strongly as the religious architecture of the parish closes studded around Brittany, especially in the Pays de Léon. A religious event totally unique to Brittany is the *pardon*, an annual religious celebration, in which people of the town join with pilgrims for a procession to honour their saint. Between May and September, hardly a day goes by without one taking place somewhere. They are earnest occasions, too, with banners and relics displayed through the streets. Ladies don their *coiffes* – tall lace headdresses shaped like the menhirs that dot the countryside. After the procession, there is usually some Breton music and a fair. Local tourist offices will be able to supply more details.

Legends

City dwellers who visit Brittany often have to suspend their big-city cynicism. The region is steeped in folklore, legends and stories, which are lent imaginative force by a sea-battered landscape frequently shrouded in mist. Bretons love to dwell on the magic mysticism of demons and fairies, however incredible and implausible they may seem to non-believers.

There's the legend of Gradlon, the King of Cornouaille, and the lost City of Ys. When the king's daughter Dahut made love with the Devil, in the guise of a handsome young man, the latter promptly opened the sluice gates of Ys and the city was drowned forever beneath Douarnenez Bay. Gradlon escaped on horseback, pushing his daughter back into the waves. She was transformed into a mermaid and today lures unwary sailors to their watery graves. There's Ankou, the coachman of death – the grim reaper with his scythe – tirelessly travelling around Brittany, and *korrigans* (sea elves), who have been spotted dancing on the waves.

Perhaps Brittany's most famous legend is that of King Arthur and his knights in the ancient forest of Brocéliande (now the Forêt de Paimpont, west of Rennes), from where Arthur is believed to have ruled England sometime in the 5th or 6th century. This is the forest where Merlin the Welsh wizard helped the young Arthur pull the magic sword *Excalibur* from the stone, and where he himself was enchanted by Viviane.

Of course there is no hard evidence to support any of these tales. Like all folklore, beliefs have little to do with facts, and time inevitably embosses its importance. In Brittany, however, you tend to believe what you like.

FESTIVALS

Some nautical festivals (*fêtes de la mer*) take place in these locations on the following dates each year:
Lancieux – 24–26 July
St-Malo (*son et lumière*) – 25 July
Locquémeau – 26 July
Port Louis/Lorient – 24–26 July
Pleumeur-Bodou – 7–9 August
St-Malo (*son et lumière*) – 8 and 14 August
La-Trinité-sur-Mer/Le Bono – 15 August
Concarneau – 16 August
Cancale – 22–23 August

Breton music continues to enjoy great popularity in the region.

BRETON DANCING CLASSES

Are you out of step with Bretons and want to know how it's done properly? A summer school of traditional Breton and Irish dancing at Mantallot on the northern coast of Brittany will arrange accommodation and food as well as dancing lessons, walks and storytelling evenings. Details from **Kanfarted ar Vilin Gozh**, Mairie, Mantallot, France 22450; tel: 96.35.89.84.

MUSIC FESTIVALS

Lorient, 6–15 August, **Fête Interceltique** (Inter-Celtic Festival) is the biggest Celtic music event in Brittany, with thousands of Celtic artists.
Quimper, 21–26 July, **Fête de la Cornouaille** Celtic music festival.
Concarneau, 29 July–3 August, folk festival.
St-Malo, 1–2 August, jazz festival.
Lamballe, 1–2 August, folk festival.
Sarzeau, first fortnight in August, art and music festival.
Belle-Ile, 11–14 August, island festival.
Trégastel, mid-August, sailing spectacle, with Breton jazz and rock groups playing on the quayside.

Music

A loud solo chant, evoking emotive rural tales of times past, usually signifies the start of a Breton song. The singer is likely to be joined by musicians playing a *bombard*, a wooden wind instrument with a double reed, a *biniou*, a Breton bagpipe, a *telenn*, a Celtic harp, and any number of other musicians playing flutes, clarinets, fiddles and an Irish drum. Inspired by the themes and instrumental styles common to the Celtic heritage, Breton music has historically exercised a potent unifying force throughout the region. Its popularity is much in evidence at any number of cultural events, including a *bœuf*. This is a feast of Celtic music, usually impromptu, performed by a group of local musicians, who will sit and play right through the night in the bar.

Fest-Noz

A rich part of Breton cultural tradition and village life is the *fest-noz* (night festival), when hundreds of people come together to dance all night in huge circles, linked only by their hands, arms or little fingers, their movements keeping in perfect rhythm to the rousing music. In summer *festou-noz* are very popular, and are usually held outdoors in the grounds of ancient châteaux, chapel courtyards and village squares. They are also held in winter, so look out for signs in local newspapers or bill posters.

SPORT AND RECREATION
In and On the Water

The best beaches for **swimming** are located at La Baule near Nantes, and in the Pays de Bigouden, especially in Loctudy and Beg-Meil. The beaches facing the Golfe de Morbihan are also particularly good, as are those on Brittany's northern resorts along the Côte d'Emeraude and Côte de Granit Rose.

Water-skiing is another popular aquatic sport. Most resorts in Brittany have a wide channel at right angles to the coast, where boats can beach at a speed of 5 knots. In main resorts boats and equipment will be available for hire at a reasonable cost.

There are numerous **sub-aqua diving** clubs in Brittany, offering courses and activities for beginners. More experienced divers might like to explore the underwater archaeological sights at Er Lanic in the Golfe de Morbihan. For more information, contact Pays de la Loire de la Fédération Française d'Etudes et Sports Sous-Marins, 78 rue Ferdinand Buisson, 44600 St-Nazaire, tel: 40.70.79.20.

Windsurfing equipment is usually available for hire at major and many smaller beaches, and in addition there are often schools providing instruction. Generally, you're not allowed to go further than 1.6km (1 mile) off shore, and it is courteous to keep out of the way of bathers.

Each major Breton port – Paimpol, for example – has a **sailing** school that hires out sailing boats and runs courses for novices and more experienced sailors.

Golf

Beaches are not the only place to find sand in Brittany, as the region has an impressive array of nine- and 18-hole courses. On the Côte d'Emeraude, the best

---

LIFE'S A BEACH

A selection of Brittany's best beaches:
St-Malo – its long expanse of golden sand is one of the best on Brittany's northern Channel coast.
Pléneuf-Val-André: a curving, golden, sandy beach on the Côte d'Emeraude – without doubt one of the finest beaches in Brittany.
Trégastel: pale pink sands strewn with boulders on the Côte de Granit Rose.
Le Pouldu: three large, excellent, south-facing beaches with dunes, between Lorient and Pont-Aven.
Bénodet: dozens of good beaches not far south of Quimper.
Carnac: not all standing stones – nearby Carnac-Plage has fine sandy beaches, too.
La Baule: this huge sandy beach west of Nantes is Brittany's most popular resort.

Gentle exercise on one of Dinard's three sandy beaches.

INFORMATION FOR CYCLISTS

Having very few hills, Brittany is gentle cycling country. Further information for two-wheeled visitors is available from **Ligue de Bretagne de Cyclotourisme**, 5 Lotissement Belle-Vue, 56250 St-Nolff, tel: 97.45.42.54.

BOULED OVER

All over Brittany it can seem as though every available square metre of flat sand is taken up with Breton men in peaked caps playing *boules*, their faces a picture of studied concentration. Although some will never admit to it, many are playing a version of the game called *apéritif*, in which the losers have to pay for the drinks after the game.

A mouthwatering seafood platter – there's plenty to stimulate the appetite in Brittany.

courses are at Dinard, St-Briac-sur-Mer, Pleumeur-Bodou, Sables d'Or-Fréhel and St-Cast-le-Guildo. The St-Malo-Le Tronchet course is 38km (24 miles) south of St-Malo. Almost as if to remind you that you're in Brittany, there are megaliths in the bunkers of the 16th and 18th holes. An **Armor Green Pass** allows golfers in the Côtes d'Armor to choose four courses from six in a one-week period. For more details, tel: 96.62.72.15, fax: 96.33.59.10.

Horse-riding

You don't have to sign up for a specialized horse-riding course to experience the joys of the saddle. There are signposted tracks throughout Brittany and dozens of clubs exist. Information on horse-riding is available from the **Association Régionale de Tourisme Equestre en Bretagne**, 1 rue Gambetta, 56300 Pontivy. A full list of horse-riding centres is available from the **Ligue Equestre de Bretagne**, 16 rue Georges Collier, 56103 Lorient.

FOOD AND DRINK

From delicious pâtisseries, lightly dusted with icing sugar, to flat-shelled Bélon oysters, Breton cuisine is as varied and imaginative as the region itself. Many of Brittany's food specialities are famous around the world. Its farm butter is of exceptional quality and its round tins of pâté, made by Henaff, have been popular and practical standbys for generations of sailors.

If shellfish, seafood and crustaceans whet your appetite then you're in for a treat. Mussels, oysters and clams are all farmed on Brittany's coast, as are lobsters, spider crabs and langoustines, especially in the area around Pont-l'Abbé in Finistère. There are many different kinds of fish caught each day in the ports around Brittany's coast, ranging from whiting, mackerel, sole, hake and sardines. Salmon and trout can be readily found in Brittany's inland rivers.

If you're not so keen on fish, you're hardly likely to starve. Morlaix is famous for its meat, notably its ham and sausages (*andouilles* or *andouillettes*). Duck is popular in Nantes, chicken in Rennes, and crêperies are to be seen everywhere.

Far breton *tastes just as good as it looks.*

Fish and Seafood

With 1200km (750 miles) of coastline to fish, naturally Brittany specializes in seafood and shellfish, and there is an enormous variety to choose from, including *palourdes* (stuffed clams), prawns, oysters, scallops, cockles, mussels, eels and crabs.

Specialities are cooked in interesting sauces, including *beurre blanc*, a sauce using cream and butter mixed with wine, vinegar and shallots. *Homard à l'armoricaine* is Brittany's best known lobster dish, cooked in a rich cream, shallot, tomato, white wine and cognac sauce. Restaurants all over the world serve it as lobster *à l'américaine*, a corruption of the ancient name for Brittany. In their defence they claim that the dish was invented in a Paris restaurant at the request of an American customer. Indecisive palates should order seafood platters or the Breton equivalent of *bouillabaisse* – a mix between a fish soup and stew called *cotriade*, based around conger eel but with other local seafood thrown in. The dish has come a long way since it started life as a simple fisherman's supper.

And, of course, Brittany is renowned for its oysters (*huîtres*), the most famous of which can be found around Cancale Bay, near St-Malo, a small port devoted to them.

SWEET TOOTH

Visitors to Brittany with a sweet tooth should look out for the following cakes and pastries:
Far breton – a rich baked custard tart flavoured with rum and often with raisins or prunes.
Far sac'h – butter-rich plum pudding.
Kouign-amann – pronounced 'Queen Amman', a delicious crispy Breton cake made from butter layered with sugar from Douarnenez.
Sables bretons – butter biscuits.
Tom-ha-ynn (literally, hot and cold) – a hot white-flour crêpe stuffed with cold vanilla ice cream and covered with hot chocolate.
Crêpes dentelles – extremely thin wafer biscuits from Quimper (*dentelle* means lace).
Craquelins – sweets from St-Malo.

Cancale is Brittany's oyster capital. Quay-side stalls offer a fresh selection daily.

Bretons love to argue over which oysters are superior – the flat-shelled Bélons or the teardrop-shaped *creuses*.

How to Eat an Oyster

Ultimately, as you've bought them, you can eat oysters how you like, but fear of embarrassment means that many people never get past the opening stage.

You don't need to apply for an open-learning course – follow these directions and you should have no problem. The trick is to cut the oyster's muscle and twist open to prise the shell apart, without getting any of the shell fragments in the opened oyster.

Hold the oyster in a thick cloth to protect your hand, with the flatter side and hinge facing you. Don't try to open it at the hinge – insert the tip of an oyster knife (any knife with a strong blade will be fine) at the muscle, located two-thirds up from the hinge. When the muscle has been severed, put the knife into the hinge, twisting the knife back and forth between the shell, and prise it apart. Remove the top shell before cutting the oyster free.

If the oysters are really fresh they should smell of the sea and cringe when lemon juice is squeezed on them. If they're off, your nose will soon let you know about it. With the hard work done, all you have to worry about is how to eat them.

Traditionally, oysters are eaten raw with just a touch of lemon juice, although some people prefer a little vinegar. Now tip the oyster into your mouth and swallow only when you get the full taste.

A dozen oysters and a glass of white wine are reputed to be a good cure for a hangover. They are traditionally regarded as an aphrodisiac, and oyster-opening skills as a test of virility.

KNOW YOUR OYSTERS

Bélons – flat-shelled oysters from the south of Brittany.
Pieds de Cheval – quite expensive, shaped like a horse's hoof (hence their name).
Creuses – generally cheaper, teardrop-shaped hollow oysters imported from Portugal and Japan.

Other Regional Dishes

Travel to inland Brittany and seafood cuisine soon
moves to the back-burner. Many traditional Breton
dishes, such as *kouign patates* (potato cake), derive from
potatoes, first introduced to the island of Belle-Ile in the
18th century by Irish refugees. Also a source of cooking,
not to mention exports, are vegetables such as
cauliflowers, artichokes, onions, turnips and cabbages.

As for meat, sheep reared on the salt marshes near
Mont-St-Michel provide a high-quality lamb called *pré-
salé*, a delicacy when served with white beans. And
Chateaubriand, beef cut from the thickest fillet, is named
after the famous author who was brought up at
Combourg castle and who is buried at St-Malo.

Créperies, serving buckwheat pancakes (once the
main sustenance of poor Breton farmers) with a choice of
sweet and savoury fillings, are ubiquitous. If you go
more than twenty paces in a town without seeing one
you must have strayed out of Brittany. *Galettes* are *crêpes*
in eastern Brittany, where they are generally thicker and
preferred with savoury fillings. Bretons think nothing of
eating *crêpes* filled with ham, egg and cheese perhaps,
followed by one filled with chocolate or honey for
dessert. No doubt you'll come to agree with them.

Brittany's locally produced wine – Muscadet or *Gros
Plant*, both dry whites
grown south of the Loire in
the Nantes region – goes
well with seafood,
especially oysters. But old
habits die hard and many
Bretons traditionally favour
cider with their meal, with
locals preferring coarse
farmer's cider in pottery
mugs. And with Breton
butter at the base of so
much of its cuisine, only the
foolhardy go to Brittany
hoping to lose weight.

FAUX AMIS

Some French words may look
familiar, but their meaning is
not always what you might
expect. To avoid
misunderstanding (and
sometimes embarrassment),
make sure you use the right
word to order what you
want.
Lard – not animal fat, but
bacon; it's a popular filling in
galettes.
Persil – not a well-known
brand of washing powder,
but the herb, parsley.
Préservatifs – not
something used in jam-
making, but condoms!

*Open markets are a
colourful feature of Breton
life, often selling locally
grown fruit and vegetables.*

2
Ille-et-Vilaine

Not quite Breton, not quite French, Ille-et-Vilaine is a puzzling hybrid. It's the least Breton of the region's four *départements* and yet, like the rest of Brittany, it radiates from every corner a feeling of *dépaysement*, a sense of separateness from the rest of France.

There is less than 160km (100 miles) along its northern Atlantic coast; it has no parish closes, few calvaries, very few *pardons* and fewer still megaliths. But its inhabitants still speak French with a Breton accent.

And the spell of the sea and Breton maritime traditions are still here, too. Even in the dense wooded areas of the *Argoat* (inland), you are never more than 95km (60 miles) from the north or south coast – even when you are under the spell of the legends of King Arthur and Merlin in the **Forêt de Paimpont**, west of Brittany's capital, **Rennes**, a lively city with a cosmopolitan feel.

The department's central area is one of inland green valleys, woods and heathlands, dotted with small towns and lakes. To the east are a number of fortified medieval frontier towns that once protected Brittany's border with Normandy, and other castles built for no other reason than to improve a family's social standing. The castles of **Fougères** and **Vitré** still inspire awe, while the megalithic sites of **Dol-de-Bretagne** are similarly impressive.

And there are some unforgettable towns to visit – from the rebellious port and one-time pirate stronghold of **St-Malo**, the majestic **Mont-St-Michel** (now in Normandy, but still a magnet for visitors), to the faded elegance of chic **Dinard**, just across the Rance estuary.

ILLE-ET-VILAINE CLIMATE

Coastal resorts are prone to cooling maritime breezes, which can reduce the temperature appreciably even on the warmest summer days. Temperatures can reach as high as 20°C (70°F) in the summer months, and winters are generally mild, with very few instances of snow.

Opposite: *Signs of a bygone age. The half-timbered houses and narrow streets of Rennes are quintessentially Breton.*

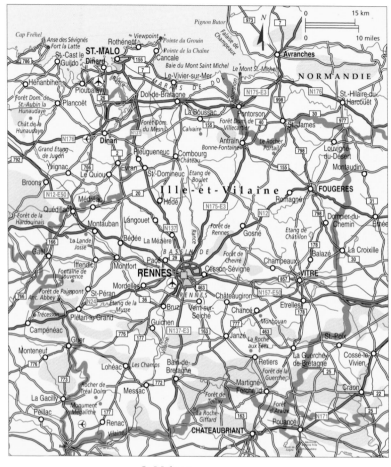

St-Malo ★★

There is no better entry point into Brittany than St-Malo, although the town is far from representative of the region, as its inhabitants are not French, not even Breton, but Malouins. If many Bretons feel independent of the rest of France, Malouins feel the same way about Brittany. It's a proud and resilient town – and for four years in the 16th century St-Malo was even an independent republic. It also makes a good base.

Opposite: *Pleasure boats dock at the foot of the ramparts in St-Malo's yacht harbour. The town's commercial port is one of France's busiest.*

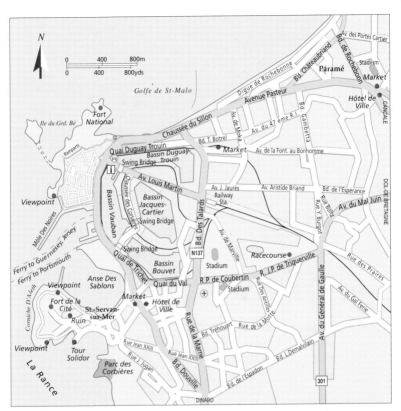

N

| 0 | 400 | 800m |
| 0 | 400 | 800yds |

Golfe de St-Malo

Av. des Portes Cartier

Bd. de Rochebonne

Bd. Châteaubriand

Paramé

Stadium

Market

CANCALE

Digue de Rochebonne

Avenue Pasteur

Hôtel de Ville

Ile du Grd. Bé

Fort National

Chaussée du Sillon

Av. de Moka

Bd. Gambetta

Av. du 47 ème R.I.

Bd. T. Botrel

Quai Duguay Trouin

Bassin Duguay-Trouin

Market

Av. de la Font. au Bonhomme

DOL-DE-BRETAGNE

Swing Bridge

Ramparts

Viewpoint

Av. Louis Martin

Chaussée des Corsaires

Bassin Vauban

Bassin Jacques-Cartier

Av. J. Jaurès

Railway Sta.

Av. Aristide Briand

Bd. de l'Espérance

Rue Y. Burgot

Rue Boltz

Av. du Mal Juin

Môle Des Noires

Swing Bridge

Bd. Des Talards

Av. de Marville

Ferry to Guernesey, Jersey

Swing Bridge

N137

Bassin Bouvet

Stadium

R.P. de Coubertin

Racecourse

R. J.P. de Triquerville

Rue des Prairies

Ferry to Portsmouth

Quai de Trichet

Quai du Val

Stadium

Rue Des Antilles

Av. du Général de Gaulle

Viewpoint

Anse Des Sablons

Market

Hôtel de Ville

Fort de la Cité

St.-Servan-sur-Mer

Ruin

Corniche D'Aleth

Rue de la Marne

Bd. Tréhouart

Rue de la Motte

Av. du Gal Ferié

Viewpoint

Tour Solidor

Parc des Corbières

Rue Jean XXIII

Rue J. Jugan

Rue Jean XXIII

Bd. Douville

Bd. L. Demalvilain

La Rance

Bd. de l'Espadon

DINARD

301

Considering its swashbuckling history, perhaps the most suitable flag to hoist above the town would be the Jolly Roger. St-Malo is nicknamed *Cité Corsaire* after its host of 17th- and 18th-century pirates, licensed by the king but largely autonomous, who preyed on foreign maritime forces, claiming their riches for themselves. However, it was the ship-owners (*armateurs*) who grew the richest, taking two-thirds of the proceeds and living in St-Malo's smartest tall houses.

St-Malo is the most visited place in the entire Breton peninsula – ironic, as you're not in Brittany proper yet. It's a lively place and you'll need a heart as hard as the granite from the Iles de Chausey to resist its charm.

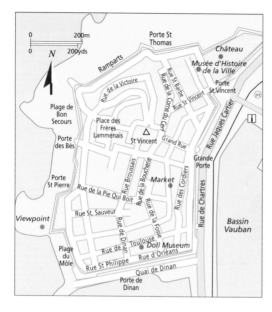

DON'T MISS

** **St-Malo**: this former pirate stronghold is the best entry point into Brittany
** **Dinard**: smart seaside town just across the Rance from St-Malo
*** **Mont-St-Michel**: just over the border in Normandy; go early to see the most inspiring sight in France
*** **Vitré**: this imposing fortress town doesn't need any drama lessons
** **Rennes**: Brittany's capital, a vibrant and youthful city
*** **Forêt de Paimpont**: lose yourself in this ancient and mysterious forest, home of the legends of King Arthur, Merlin and the Knights of the Round Table.

Old City

Originally a settlement for the Gauls, then the Romans, St-Malo is named after the Welsh monk Maclow or Maclou (Malouins dropped pronunciation of the 'c'), who settled there in the 6th century to convert the inhabitants from their pagan beliefs to Christianity. The walled section **Intra-Muros** (Latin for 'within the walls') takes up barely 24ha (59 acres) and its busy port is tucked out of sight. St-Malo originally consisted only of the fortified island of Intra-Muros, but it was later linked to the mainland by a causeway in the 18th century. In summer – July and August especially – it's a fashionable resort and the narrow cobbled streets are packed with people, even on early morning strolls amid the sweet aroma of freshly made pâtisseries and strong coffee.

A stronghold for German troops during World War II, 80% of St-Malo was wrecked in August 1944 when General Patton's 8th Army bombarded the town for two weeks to force a German surrender. During its reconstruction (using nearby Iles de Chausey granite) it was faithfully restored to its origins and today only a trained eye can see the joins between the old and new.

Just below the steps beside **Porte St-Thomas**, you'll notice a fishtank built into the 13th-century ramparts. Waxworks figures recount the deeds of St-Malo's swashbuckling heroes in the museum in the tower of **Quic-en-Groigne**, built in the 15th century by Duke Jean V of Brittany – more, some believe, to keep an eye on the Malouins than to protect them from an invasion. (The

A statue of Robert Surcouf, one of St-Malo's several famous offspring. He acquired an enormous fortune as a privateer, licensed by the king to attack and despoil warships without risk of being hanged as a pirate.

TABLE MANNERS

Disagreements in St-Malo were settled rather differently in the time of the Malouin corsairs, the most famous of whom were Robert Surcouf and René Duguay-Trouin (who captured Rio de Janeiro from Portugal in 1711). One night in a St-Malo restaurant, Surcouf is reputed to have overheard 12 Prussian officers insult his country. Incensed, he promptly challenged all of them to a duel. He killed 11 men, but spared the last officer so that word of his deeds could be spread. Fortunately, no such cavalier attitude exists towards visitors these days.

name, incidentally, translates as 'complain who will'.) Close to **Porte St-Vincent**, the huge main gate of the town, the **Musée d'Histoire de la Ville** (open daily except Tuesday, 09:30–12:00, 14:00–18:30) wallows in St-Malo's illustrious past, from the exploits of Malouin voyagers such as Mahé La Bourdonnais and Jacques Cartier, who lived and sailed from St-Malo and discovered Canada in 1534, naming it after an Indian word for village. The town's explorers were also responsible for the Argentinian name for the Falkland Islands, Las Malvinas, after the Malouins who discovered it.

The huge spire that towers above the rampart walls belongs to the **Cathédrale St-Vincent**, built in the 12th century but restored after World War II. On sunny days light through its modern stained-glass windows provides a free colourful light show.

ANIMAL MAGIC?

During your walk around St-Malo, keep an eye open for some interesting street names. Imagine the creatures that inspired rue du Chat qui Danse (Dancing Cat Street) and rue de la Pie qui Boit (Drinking Magpie Street).

Built in 1382, the 27m (89ft) Tour Solidor in St-Servan-sur-Mer affords fine views over the Rance estuary.

Along the Ramparts

A walk along St-Malo's ramparts will take no more than an hour. There is plenty to see out at sea, like the islet of **Grand Bé**, where the St-Malo-born Romantic writer Chateaubriand is buried in a modest tomb, which can be visited at low tide. If it's a swim you want, go through the Porte St-Pierre for the **Plage de Bon Secours**, which has a public swimming pool built into the shore.

Also out at sea is **Fort National**, an island fortress that once served as a look-out post to defend the Malouins from Dutch and British seeking retribution for harassment of their ships. Built in 1689, it is today sometimes used for meetings by state officials, and some have been spotted by locals paddling ashore with rolled-up trousers and carrying their shoes when business ended later than expected.

St-Malo Suburbs

In high season when accommodation is hard to come by in St-Malo, you might want to try cheaper out-of-the-way hotels in **Paramé**, to the east towards Cancale. It's a rather uninspiring suburb of St-Malo, but it does have a 3km (2-mile) sandy beach (Grande Plage).

You cannot fail to notice the triple towers of the 14th-century **Tour Solidor** in St-Servan-sur-Mer (formerly called Aleth), a neighbouring fishing resort, popular for its huge beach and marina. The tower was built by a succession of French monarchs to try and keep the rebellious Malouins in line. Set on a small promontory, it houses a museum of memorabilia dedicated to Cape Horn sailors, including Captain Cook and Sir Francis Drake.

Dinard ★★

Over the mouth of the Rance oppo-site St-Malo lies the chic town of Dinard. A 10-minute ferry trip (in summer only; buses run off season) will take you to a place that was just a humble fishing village until the late 19th century, when British Victorian high society was keen to establish for itself a little Brighton rather than sample Breton life. Suddenly it became all the rage for aristocratic entrepreneurs to send their families to a healthy resort abroad with fresh air and sea breezes. Inevitably, the middle classes followed, bringing with them all their heirs and graces. Their ostentatious villas – mock-Tudor manors, ornate mini-palaces – still line the cliffs that overlook the Rance estuary and St-Malo Bay.

Walking along the beach can be an enjoyably tranquil experience in Dinard.

With a casino, terraced gardens and Grecian urns still maintaining its air of wealth, Dinard is also a popular centre for sports and activities, especially on its three good sandy beaches, one of which is the orange-sanded Plage de l'Ecluse. There's also an attractive coastal path along the Promenade du Clair de Lune that leads to the Pointe du Moulinet, from where there are good views over to St-Malo on the right, and Cap Fréhel on the left.

EAST TO CANCALE

Further along the coast east of St-Malo, **Rothéneuf** has some unusual sculpted rocks (*rochers sculptés*). The rocks, carved into a bizarre assortment of animal, vegetable and human shapes, are the life's work of a 19th-century priest. Just south of the **Pointe du Grouin**, the finger of land and wildlife sanctuary that points towards the Channel Islands, **Cancale** is a charmingly pretty fishing port that is also Brittany's oyster capital. Less than 15km (9^1/2 miles)

ACTIVITY HOLIDAY?

There are plenty of sports and activities available in St-Malo. Bicycles can be hired from **Cycles Diazo**, 47 quai Duguay-Trouin (tel: 99.40.31.63) or **Cycles Nicole**, 11 rue Robert-Schumann (tel: 99.56.11.06). If you feel like windsurfing, you can hire boards from **Surf School**, 7 rue Courtoisville (tel: 99.40.07.47) or the **Centre de Voile**, quai du Bajoyer (tel: 99.40.84.42).

*Many visitors are attracted
to Cancale for its oysters,
which are cultivated from
year-old spats in vast beds
known as* parcs à huîtres.
*Both the hollow oyster
(*creuse*), of Japanese
origin, and the native flat
Bélon oyster are grown
here.*

FOOTPATHS ON THE COAST

There is a good walk
between Cancale and St-
Malo on the GR34 coastal
footpath, a route favoured by
coastguards. Keep your eyes
peeled for look-out points
and old military emplace-
ments en route.

LA POINTE DU GROUIN

This rocky point juts out further than any other along the
northern coast of Ille-et-
Vilaine. It is 600m (1968ft)
long and 150m (492ft) wide,
and offers excellent views of
the Bay of Mont-St-Michel.

---

east of St-Malo, it has the distinction of serving top
restaurants in Paris and further afield (oysters from
Cancale used to be delivered daily to Louis XIV at
Versailles). But on the beach you'll see them being sold in
baskets (*bourriches*) or individually (*au détail*) from stalls.
Cancale's main square is lined with oyster restaurants,
but they also serve delicate cutlets of *pré-salé* lamb from
the nearby salt marshes. Many bars offer oysters and half
a bottle of Muscadet to wash them down. At low tide
from the rue des Parcs next to the port's jetty, you can see
the *parcs à huîtres* where oysters are grown and watch the
process that removes mud and impurities. The oyster
beds are extensive, covering an area of 728ha (1800 acres)
and producing upwards of 25,000 tons of oysters a year.
An oyster museum (Musée de l'Huître et du Coquillage)
located in the Saint Kerber gardens in Cancale describes
all the different kinds available (tel: 99. 89. 69. 99.).

Cancale offers a few other attractions besides its oysters. There are footpaths to explore, and the **Sentier des
Douaniers** (Customs Path) leads as far as St-Malo, via
the Pointe du Grouin and Rothéneuf.

The coast around the old fishing port of **Le-Vivier-
sur-Mer** is a huge mussel-growing centre, the largest in
France, harvesting tens of thousands each year from distinctive mussel-encrusted *bouchots* (poles) that stretch
into the sea for what seems like eternity – or until they
reach the port of Cancale, at any rate.

Mont-St-Michel ★★★

Further to the east of Cancale, just past the border with Normandy at Pontorson, lies the stunning spectacle of Mont-St-Michel, the most famous sight in France outside Paris. Only bats flying around the spire of the abbey could make it look more like a set for a horror film.

Essentially, Mont-St-Michel is a small town perched on a rock platform 1.6km (1 mile) offshore, with narrow, cobbled streets leading up to its now famous 8th-century Romanesque and Gothic **abbey**. Although technically in Normandy, Mont-St-Michel is still as synonymous with Brittany as *galettes* and the *coiffe* headdresses worn by old women in the Pays de Bigouden. However, the rush of its tides has, over the centuries, changed the course of the Couesnon river, which traditionally marks the frontier with Normandy. So the Bretons may have lost the mound, but they still have the huge sweep of Mont-St-Michel Bay, home to acres of oyster beds, mussels and notoriously quick tides and quicksands, as well as sheep reared on salt marshes, later sold as *pré-salé* lamb, which is considered a delicacy throughout the region.

> **TOURS OF MONT-ST-MICHEL BAY**
>
> The red-sailed oyster *bisquines* that inspired Claude Debussy to write *La Mer* no longer sail around this coast, but a restored version offers trips around the bay. Contact the **Association de la Bisquine Cancalaise** (tel: 99.89.88.87). Also based at Le Vivier-sur-Mer is *La Sirène de la Baie*, a 29m (90ft) amphibious vehicle that takes passengers across the sand and sea of Mont-St-Michel Bay, visiting offshore beds growing oysters and mussels. Trips last 90 minutes and include a gastronomic lunch (12:30) or dinner (20:30); for details tel: 99.48.82.30.

Dubbed 'the Marvel of the Western world', Mont-St-Michel is the most awe-inspiring sight in France, rising impressively above the flatness of the surrounding coastal plain. As the sea retreats, up to 15km (9 miles) of sand are exposed; the incoming tide is said to move at the speed of a galloping horse.

NOMINOE

Dol-de-Bretagne is famous for being the site where Nominoë, supreme Breton chieftain, was crowned first Duke of Brittany in the 9th century. While books may extol the deeds of other Breton leaders, beware of imitators – if there is a Breton hero, Nominoë is the man. His claim to fame is that he was the first to unify the Breton tribes into a powerful entity, and he subsequently became the first leader of an independent Brittany.

Mont-St-Michel is reached via a causeway across the bay, and a brisk climb up a narrow twisting street leads to the abbey itself, access to which is strictly by guided tour. Built over a period of five centuries, the abbey nevertheless presents a graceful and harmonious whole that never fails to inspire awe (it was given the epithet *La Merveille*, the marvel, in the 13th century).

Inevitably, Mont-St-Michel has been excessively commercialized and is now a magnet for tourists. However fairy-tale or dream-like it looks, endless coaches of day-trippers will soon bring you back to reality, even off season. Your best bet is to go *very early* in the morning.

Dol-de-Bretagne

The former religious capital of Brittany for 1300 years, **Dol-de-Bretagne** 30km (18 miles) west of Mont-St-Michel makes for a good day trip. Its impressive cathedral is not the original, but was built to replace an earlier structure that King John of England had burned to the ground in 1203. It is a superb building with beautiful stained-glass windows depicting scenes from the life of St Sansom. The **Musée d'Histoire et d'Art Populaire** in the town is worth a visit for its collection of religious statuary. The town also has a number of ancient houses.

One of the several locks along the Ille-et-Rance canal between the peaceful villages of Hédé and Tinténiac.

Many legends surround the megalith sites just south of the town. The **Menhir du Champ-Dolent**, a standing stone nearly 9m (30ft) tall, is believed to have been dropped from the sky to break up two brothers on the verge of killing each other. But with all legends there is always more than one theory, and another says that the menhir is slowly inching its way into the ground, and that when it finally disappears the world will end. Until the 12th century, **Mont Dol** to the north of Dol-de-Bretagne was an island when the sea reached this far inland. There are some good views towards Mont-St-Michel from the top of this 65m (208ft) granite escarpment. The **Forêt de Ville-Cartier**, a pine and beech forest south of Dol, is superb walking country.

The tenth child of a noble Breton family, François-René de Chateaubriand was born in St-Malo in 1768, though he spent part of his formative years in Combourg castle.

SOUTH OF DOL-DE-BRETAGNE

A short distance to the south lies the feudal **Château de Combourg**, where melancholic writer René de Chateaubriand spent his childhood. Despite being beautifully reflected in its large lake, the castle is said to have been responsible for much of the author's gloom.

The castle is meant to be haunted by a cat, although Chateaubriand claimed it was possessed by the wooden leg of a previous landlord. The writer's former living quarters – the Tour du Chat – are now partly a museum, open to visitors during the summer.

The main road south to Rennes (N137) passes the old village of **Tinténiac**, which is dominated by flowers. Further south, **Hédé** is surrounded by some attractive countryside and has its own ruined castle. There are many locks on the Ille-et-Rance canal between Hédé and Tinténiac, leading south to the Atlantic coast.

EARTH MOTHERS?

There is an interesting passage grave called the House of Fairies located southwest of Dol-de-Bretagne in the **Forêt du Mesnil** (Mesnil Forest) near the village of Tressé, close to Combourg. Perfectly preserved, the grave is covered by seven slabs of granite, but on the stones supporting the roof are engraved eight pairs of breasts, topped by necklaces, believed to be early symbols of an Earth Mother Goddess cult characteristic of the period when it was built – approximately 2500BC.

FOUGERES' MANUFACTURING HISTORY

Fougères has made its living in many different ways over the years. In the 14th century it was an important weaving town; cloth was the mainstay in the 15th century, linen in the 16th, and glass-blowing in the 17th century. From the 19th century until the start of World War I the town became a centre for the manufacture of women's shoes.

A short drive west of Tinténiac on the D20, the **Château de Caradeuc** is located just outside the ancient fortified town of **Bécherel**, perched on top of a hill. With its lavish gardens (*jardin à la française*) and pyramid-shaped yew trees, this elegantly landscaped park merits its status as the Breton equivalent of Versailles.

Fougères **

It is easy to feel intimidated by the sheer magnitude of Fougères, the first and most impressive of the defensive line of castles along Brittany's eastern frontier with Normandy, the site of constant battle in the Middle Ages. It remains a fine example of a medieval fortress.

The noble towers of the triangular-shaped **château** were the inspiration both for Victor Hugo and for Balzac's *Les Chouans*, which describes the Breton attempt to restore the monarchy after the French Revolution. Fougères castle is believed to be the largest in western Europe.

Fougères town is built around its massive château, which is located in a valley rather than on top of a hill, using the waters of the Nançon river nearby to fill its large moat. Fougères was repeatedly under siege during the Hundred Years' War, details of which can be found in the castle **museum**. The castle was rebuilt after it was first burned down in 1166 by the king of England, Henry

La Roche-aux-Fées (Fairies' Rock) is the biggest megalithic monument in Brittany, probably constructed in 2500BC and consisting of 42 purple schist stones. The site may have been a burial chamber, but its precise origins remain elusive.

Plantagenet. The outer walls with their 13 tall towers were added in the 13th century. The **forest** of Fougères, just north of town on the D177, offers some good walks among beech trees, megaliths and ruins.

West of Fougères on the N12 is **St-Aubin-du-Cormier**, a peaceful town worth visiting for its castle keep. A monument in a nearby field marks the spot where in 1488 the Breton forces of Duke François were beaten by the army of King Charles VIII of France. In the battle many of the Breton soldiers wore the English colours of a black cross on white silk to fool French generals into thinking they were the Duke's English reinforcements. Unfortunately for these Breton soldiers, French military officials gave orders to spare the Bretons, but to kill the English prisoners.

Vitré ★★★

With its narrow cobbled streets, Vitré, situated some 32km (20 miles) to the south on a ridge overlooking the Vilaine valley, is a dramatic fortress town *par excellence*. Its **château** has its own drawbridge entrance, while the machicolated towers have distinctive pointed slate-grey roofs that look like sharp pencils.

The castle was built in the 14th and 15th centuries, when the Hundred Years' War was at its most intense. English forces maintained the castle under siege for a period of several years, until paid a sizeable ransom by the castle's inhabitants to go away. The area beneath the castle that was occupied by the English is still known as **Rachapt**, a corruption of the word *rachat*, or repurchase. The suburb's old streets afford fine views of the castle.

During the Wars of Religion Vitré was a Protestant stronghold, belonging to the Huguenot Coligny family, and was besieged unsuccessfully by the Catholic League. Its only battle now is against the Côtes d'Armor town of Dinan (see page 53) for the title of Brittany's best preserved medieval fortress town. From the castle there are good views of the valley of the Vilaine. The nearby towns of **Dompierre-du-Chemin**, **Champeaux** and **Châteaubourg** are also worth exploring.

THIRD TIME UNLUCKY

A legend abounds in the town of **Dompierre-du-Chemin** near Vitré. In olden days, Charlemagne's prefect and nephew, Roland, would leap on horseback across the 100m (328ft) gap that separates the nearby valley of Cantache. After two successful attempts, on the third occasion he fell into the ravine and died. The drops of water that trickle out of the 'leaking stone' nearby are believed to be the tears of Roland's grieving lady.

SOUTH OF VITRÉ

The little country town of **La Guerche-de-Bretagne**,
about 22km (14 miles) south of Vitré, has an interesting
13th-century collegiate church with Renaissance glass
and sculptured choir stalls. In the 15th century La
Guerche was captured by the Duke of Somerset.

West of La Guerche in the woods near Rétiers is the
Roche-aux-Fées (Fairies' Rock), one of the best megalith
sites in all Brittany. Set on a high, exposed spot the 20m-
long (65ft) rock covers an alleyway of purple-coloured
stones. Couples are encouraged to come here on nights
when there is a new moon and count the stones separate-
ly. If both partners come up with the same number, the
prospects look good for a wedding.

Rennes ★★

After centuries of rivalry with Nantes, Rennes, in the
heart of Ille-et-Vilaine, is now the capital of Brittany. It is

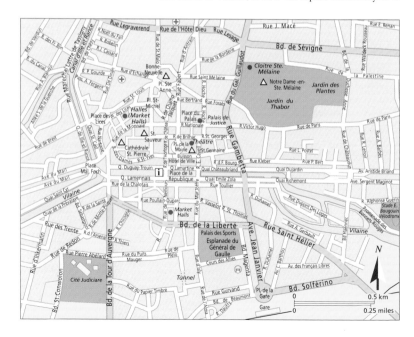

a vibrant city with a young population; a quarter of Rennes' inhabitants are students attending its two universities. Its multicultural street life and lively theatre artists from all round the world give it a cosmopolitan edge other Breton cities cannot match.

But Rennes has a maturity that belies its youthful vitality – handsome squares, clean streets and perfectly preserved medieval gabled houses with jutting upper floors and wooden staircases. Rennes is also a hard-working city that makes few concessions to the tourist; that means traffic congestion, concrete and all the other trappings of metropolitan life.

A drunken carpenter is to blame (or thank, depending on your view) for the way Rennes looks today. In 1720 he knocked over a candle and set Rennes ablaze, unwittingly destroying much of its ancient centre in the Great Fire, which raged for six days. Only the lively marketplace area known as **Les Lices**, dominated by half-timbered houses near the 17th-century **Palais de Justice**, was undamaged. Parisian architects were commissioned to rebuild the city using the French capital as their template – so sometimes you can be forgiven for believing that you're in Paris rather than Brittany.

Only a few houses managed to escape the great conflagration that destroyed medieval Rennes and much of the city's Breton character.

RENNES' BRETON MUSEUM

On display in the **Musée de Bretagne** in Rennes is a wide-ranging collection of pottery (*faïence*) and intriguing exhibits that illustrate the history and culture of the region. Different eras are evoked through the imaginative use of displays that show the evolution of Brittany from prehistoric through Gallo-Roman and medieval times, to life under the *ancien régime*. The gallery devoted to modern-day Brittany has a collection of everyday objects, costumes and furnishings.

Gate detail from the entrance to the Jardin du Thabor. This elevated site was occupied by the Benedictine abbey of St-Mélaine in the 16th century. The gardens were planted in the 19th century on the grounds formerly given over to the abbey's orchards.

Rennes is a city that has always smiled kindly on youth – when Les Lices was used as a jousting hall it was here that the 17-year-old warrior-knight Bertrand du Guesclin first commanded the attention of senior military officials. Now on Saturday mornings Les Lices hosts a lively open-air market.

The **Musée de Bretagne** is an absorbing introduction to the region's history, costumes and furniture, and the **Musée des Beaux-Arts** houses Breton pottery and works by Gauguin. Both are located in quai Emile Zola. Or you can visit the **law courts** (Palais de Justice) in the place du Palais, the seat of the Breton parliament since the time of Duchess Anne. The law courts' **Grande Chambre** is open every day except Tuesday 10:00–11:00 and 15:00–16:00.

Rennes is a good city in which to walk. Split in half by the Vilaine river, the most interesting streets lie north of **Les Quais** (the embankments), lined with classical buildings. But the heart of Rennes is its large **cobbled square**, the place de la Mairie, and its interesting town hall clock. Also worth a visit are the **place de la République**, timbered houses in the **rue Saint-Georges**, the Gothic church of **Saint-Germain** near the river, and the **rue de la Monnaie**, where Rennes once had its own mint.

Not far from the place du Palais are the 11ha (27-acre) **Jardin du Thabor** (Thabor gardens), which has botanical hothouses, formal gardens and a rich variety of plants.

THABOR GARDENS

The elegant gate and fence of Rennes' Thabor gardens were designed by Jean-Baptiste Martenot, one-time official architect of Rennes. He was also responsible for the Lycée and other buildings inside the Thabor gardens. The 11th-century tower and transept of Notre-Dame-en-St-Mélaine are all that remain of the original Benedictine abbey church.

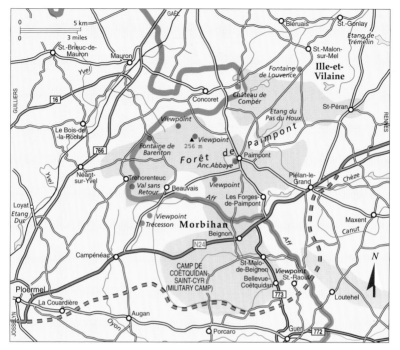

Magical Paimpont ★★★

Just inside the border of Ille-et-Vilaine 40km (25 miles) west of Rennes lies the **Forêt de Paimpont**, haunted by its magical past links with the Druids, Merlin and the court of King Arthur. Its 6880ha (17,000 acres) of oak and beech trees, a tract of land ranging over 40km² (15 sq miles) and studded with small lakes, is the last remaining forest of a vast woodland that once covered the medieval heartland of Brittany, known as the Forêt de Brocéliande. The area is rich in flora, with oak and beech in the wetlands and valleys; on drier land the terrain is mostly moorland covered with heather, gorse and broom.

This is Merlin's forest, the cradle of all legends relating to King Arthur and the Knights of the Round Table. It was here that Merlin the magician became the fairy Viviane's prisoner, and valiant knights still ride through

> ### PAIMPONT
>
> The small market town of Paimpont is an attractive settlement, situated deep in the forest amid tall trees near a woodland lake. A monastery was founded here in the 7th century, later raised to the status of abbey. Paimpont offers a good choice of accommodation and makes an excellent base from which to explore the surrounding forest.

VALLEY OF NO RETURN

In a forest already steeped in myth and magic, the Val sans Retour is probably the most heavily embroiled in Arthurian legend. It is said that Morgane the enchantress, enraged by jealousy after being jilted by a knight, cast a spell over the valley, preventing anyone guilty of infidelity from leaving it. The spell could only be broken by Lancelot, who had remained faithful to his lover, Guinevere.

the unsettling mist and tall trees of the **Val sans Retour** (Valley of No Return) in search of the fairy Morgane, who ensnared faithless lovers here. Then there is the **Barenton fountain**, where, so legend has it, anyone sprinkling a few drops of its water on a nearby rock (known as Merlin's Step) could unleash torrential rain. The fountain is said to be laughing when bubbles appear at the bottom, and visitors' wishes can be granted.

Off Route D59, near the village of Télhouet, two stone slabs mark the grave of Merlin himself, and near the impressive 15th-century **Château de Trécesson** at Campénéac is the fountain where the wizard created thunder by splashing water on a rock.

Merlin's kingdom: Paimpont forest still exercises a magical hold over all who enter it. According to medieval minstrels, this was Brocéliande, home of the enchantress Viviane and the sorcerer Merlin. The great forest that once covered most of inland Brittany has been severely depleted over the centuries, but many delightful areas such as this remain.

Although not open to the public, the castle is considered as the most beautiful château in the Forêt de Paimpont, and attracts many tourists. Surrounded by heathland, the castle's walls and turrets are reflected in its moat and it is hard not to be seduced by its charm. And if you think there's an eerie air about the castle, your suspicions may be confirmed by a legend that claims it to be haunted.

If you want to take some of the mystery out of the legend of King Arthur and the Knights of the Round Table, head for the Château de Comper-en-Brocéliande. This is said to be the birthplace of the fairy Viviane, the Lady of the Lake. The **Centre Arthurien** here presents exhibitions, audiovisuals and entertainments along the themes of the legends of the Knights of the Round Table. It can also organize guided tours of the forest of Brocéliande if required.

Redon

Founded as a religious settlement in the early 9th century, the city of Redon, in the southwest corner of Ille-et-Vilaine, continued as a place of pilgrimage until the 17th century. Its medieval church of **St-Sauveur** has a Romanesque lantern tower built from two different-coloured types of stone. In the countryside around Redon, nothing has changed for centuries, with Stone Age remains of dolmens, menhirs and stone circles.

WATERWAYS OF BRITTANY

Water in Brittany is not restricted to its fine beaches and rugged coastline. There are many inland waterways that slice through the region, providing a tranquil setting away from the sea, just waiting to be discovered.

Brittany's 660km (412 miles) of canals and waterways offer a number of possible itineraries for travellers – the north–south link connects Dinan to La Roche-Bernard on the south coast, passing Rennes and Redon. Or try the east–west route, from Nantes to Pontivy, crossing Blain, Redon, Malestroit, Josselin and Rohan. The Comité des Canaux Bretons can supply further information.

DEBUNKING THE MYTHS

The **Centre de l'Imaginaire Arthurien** is at 56430 Concoret; tel: 97.22.79.96. To get there from Rennes, take the RN24 to Paimpont, then head towards Gaël before turning right on the D31 towards St-Malon. If you're coming from the south, take the D766 and turn right to Concoret at Mauron, then take the D31 towards St-Malon.

HOLIDAYS AFLOAT

Since canals cut across areas that are inaccessible by road, Brittany's inland waterway system can take you to places that are completely wild – unofficial nature reserves, in fact. With Redon as Brittany's waterway crossroads, there are many recreation bases on the river basins of Brittany, offering comfortable houseboats for hire between spring and autumn.

Ille-et-Vilaine at a Glance

BEST TIMES TO VISIT

Like the rest of Brittany, Ille-et-Vilaine can be very over-crowded during the summer months. Booking accommodation ahead is highly recommended. Going out of season spells a huge compromise – you won't get the crowds and it will be easy just to turn up and get a hotel room, but you will also be faced with 'fermeture annuelle' signs on the doors of some hotels, restaurants and museums.

Rennes is best visited during university holidays when it is quieter, especially during August and September.

GETTING THERE

Brittany Ferries operates a daily **ferry crossing** (twice a week in winter) from Portsmouth to St-Malo (9hr). Brit Air operates daily scheduled **flights** to Rennes from London-Gatwick.

GETTING AROUND

Trains leave St-Malo station for the main junction of Rennes at hourly intervals.

Car hire is also readily available. In Rennes, established hire companies include Avis, tel: 99.30.01.19; Hertz, tel: 99.54.26.52; and Europcar, tel: 99.59.50.50.

WHERE TO STAY

St-Malo
St-Malo has a wide selection of high-standard hotels to choose from, and there's also an excellent range of lower-

cost alternatives, from chambres d'hôtes, caravan and camping sites to youth hostels. In the summer, it's essential to book ahead, as demand is great.

Hôtel Elizabeth, 2 rue des Cordiers, charming, family-run, luxury 16th-century hotel in Intra-Muros that feels loved; untouched by World War II bombardments; bed and breakfast only, no restaurant, tel: 99.56.24.98, fax: 99.56.39.24.
Hôtel Noguette, 9 rue de la Fosse, pleasant, small, reasonably priced hotel, well situated next to the central market, tel: 99.40.83.57.

Cancale
Le Chatellier, route de St-Malo, moderately priced hotel, tel: 99.89.81.84.

Dinard
Le Grand, 46 avenue George V, extremely expensive hotel with gastronomic restaurant; many rooms have superb views of the Baie de la Vicomte; has a yacht club and casino on the doorstep, tel: 99.46.10.28.
Hôtel Plage, 3 boulevard de Féart, well located, overlooking Dinard's main beach, tel: 99.46.14.87.

Mont-St-Michel
Hôtel Digue, situated 2km (1¼ miles) south from Mont-St-Michel, reasonably priced, tel: 33.60.14.02.

Fougères
Hôtel Voyageurs, 10 place de Gambetta, moderately priced, well recommended with adjacent restaurant, tel: 99.99.08.20.

Rennes
Hôtel Mercure-Centre, rue Paul-Louis Courier, modern hotel located in the former printing works of the Ouest-France newspaper, tel: 99.78.32.32.
Le Pire, 23 rue Maréchal Joffre, exclusive, expensive, much sought-after hotel, perfect for treating yourself; only four rooms, therefore advance booking is essential, tel: 99.79.31.41.

WHERE TO EAT

St-Malo
Duchesse Anne, 5 place Guy la Chambre, famous but expensive restaurant built into the ramparts, with a Michelin star, tel: 99.40.85.33.
Chez Sinbad, Marché aux Légumes, small, well-priced and friendly crêperie with good atmosphere.
L'Astrolabe, 8 rue des Cordiers, serves very good desserts, tel: 99.40.36.82.

Cancale
Le Cancalais, quai Gambetta, good food is matched by excellent views of the harbour, tel: 99.89.61.93.

Mont-St-Michel
Mouton Blanc, good value food in a historic building that

Ille-et-Vilaine at a Glance

also serves as a hotel, tel: 33.60.14.08.

La Mère Poulard, Grand-Rue, more an event than a meal, and you'll pay for the notoriety of this famous restaurant, open all year, tel: 33.60.14.01.

Dinard

Altair, 18 boulevard Féart, specializes in seafood, especially sole and *Coquilles St-Jacques* (scallops); closed Sunday evenings and Mondays, tel: 99.46.13.58.

De la Paix, 6 place de la République, serves good meat and fish dishes, closed Monday, tel: 99.46.10.38.

Rennes

Chez Kub, 20 rue du Chapitre, small, moderately priced restaurant that specializes in grilled meats, tel: 99.31.19.31.

Le Palais, 7 place du Parlement de Bretagne, quite expensive *haute cuisine*, but one of Rennes' best restaurants in a superb location, specializing in milk-fed lamb; closed Sunday evening, all Monday and the second half of August, tel: 99.79.45.01.

Vitré

Le Petit-Billot, 5 place Maréchal Leclerc, moderately priced, friendly restaurant, tel: 99.74.68.88.

Château de Fougères shoe museum: open between mid-

June and mid-September, daily 09:00–19:00 and at other times the rest of the year; tel: 99.99.79.59.

Musée International de la Faune, Québriac, near Tinténiac and Hédé: an international fauna museum that features a varied collection of stuffed animals; open Easter to November daily 14:30–18:30; December to Easter, Sunday 14:30–18:30; tel: 99.68.10.22.

Forêt de Rennes: 11km (7 miles) to the northeast of Rennes, this beautiful 3000ha (7413-acre) state-managed forest has birch, oak, beech, pine and chestnut trees and a long-distance footpath for walkers. A network of roads also crosses the forest.

Barrage de la Rance (Rance Tidal Power Station), Le Richardais, between St-Malo and Dinard: the world's only hydroelectric plant using tidal force for industrial power production, opened in 1966; tel: 99.46.21.89.

Ecomusée de la Bintinais, just south of Rennes: a folk museum exhibition of past and present farming life, spanning five centuries of rural history; audiovisual and

other displays explain the development of farming techniques as well as the skill of cider-making; tel: 99.51.38.15.

Château des Rochers, close to Vitré: once the home of Madame de Sévigné, whose letters offer a witty look at life in the Sun King's Court; tel: 99.96.76.51.

Comité Départemental du Tourisme des Ille-et-Vilaine, 1 rue de Martenot, 3500 Rennes, tel: 99.02.97.43.

St-Malo Office du Tourisme, esplanade de St-Vincent, supplies excellent maps and has a good selection of brochures, tel: 99.56.64.48.

Cancale Office du Tourisme, 44 rue du Port, tel: 99.93.00.13.

Dinard Office du Tourisme, 2 boulevard Féart, tel: 99.46.94.12.

SNCF train station, Rennes, tel: 99.65.50.50.

Bus station, Rennes, tel: 99.30.87.80.

Comité des Canaux Bretons, tel: 99.31.59.44. Supplies useful information about inland waterways and canals.

DINARD	J	F	M	A	M	J	J	A	S	O	N	D
AVERAGE TEMP. °F	41	43	45	48	54	59	63	63	63	54	48	43
AVERAGE TEMP. °C	5	6	7	9	12	15	17	17	17	12	9	6
Hours of Sun Daily	2	3	5	6	7	7	8	7	6	4	3	2
RAINFALL in	3	3	2	2	2	2	2	2	2	3	4	3
RAINFALL mm	69	64	59	49	63	47	42	43	57	74	88	72
Days of Rainfall	20	16	17	15	15	13	11	13	14	16	19	19

3
Côtes d'Armor

Known formerly as the Côtes-du-Nord, this long and extremely attractive stretch of Channel coast now enjoys the much more suitable name of Côtes d'Armor – the second half has its origins in Brittany's ancient name of Armorica, meaning 'land of the sea'.

There is medieval magic to be found in the towns of **Dinan** and **Tréguier**, where sometimes only the sight of a motor car brings you back to the 20th century. Not far away towards the coast are pretty little ports and small fishing villages such as **Paimpol**, rich in maritime history, or **Binic**, which has splendid views out to sea.

Family holidays are written in the sand along the ever-popular **Côte d'Emeraude** (Emerald Coast). The slightly surreal **Côte de Granit Rose** (Pink Granite Coast), west of Paimpol, is named after its dramatic, oddly shaped granite rocks, which are tinted pink. Its seaside resorts include **Trébeurden**, **Trégastel** and **Perros-Guirec**; the latter also specializes in the peculiarly Breton seawater treatment known as **thalassotherapy**, which enjoys great popularity in the region. The offshore island of **Ile de Bréhat** is a peaceful haven, where cars are banned and where many French families favour a holiday over other resorts, including the French Riviera.

Dinan ***

Comfortable shoes are recommended in Dinan, an old fortress town, with its medieval battlements, steep cobbled streets and leaning houses overlooking the Rance Valley. Miss it at your peril. With its 3km (2 miles) of

COTES D'ARMOR CLIMATE

Proximity to the sea inevitably means cool breezes, and a jacket or sweater is a sensible precaution in summer. Be prepared for rain at any time of the year; it's a good idea to pack a waterproof coat and sturdy shoes. Winters generally bring frost, but not usually snow.

Opposite: *Cap Fréhel, on the aptly named Emerald Coast. The cliffs rise majestically to a height of 70m (230ft), offering dramatic seascapes.*

DON'T MISS

*** Dinan: steep cobbled streets and half-timbered houses make this the most popular of Brittany's medieval walled towns
*** Pléneuf-Val-André: stunning sweeping sands along the Côte d'Emeraude
** Paimpol: a small fishing town still dreaming of its illustrious past
*** Ile de Bréhat: take a boat trip to this tranquil, car-free and carefree island
** Tréguier: attractive medieval town with an unusual stone-spired cathedral and a world-renowned *pardon*.

ramparts still intact, Dinan is the best preserved and the most visited walled citadel in Brittany.

A walk through its narrow streets of 15th- and 16th-century houses, with their half-timbered upper storeys and steep gables, provides a real insight into the kinds of jobs people had in days gone by – all are named after medieval trades: rue de la Poissonerie (fishmonger); rue de la Ferronnerie (ironmonger); place des Merciers (haberdasher); place des Cordeliers (Franciscan friars); rue de l'Horloge (clockmaker).

Dinan's **Jardin anglais** (English gardens) allow superb views of the medieval town and the River Rance. Just behind the gardens is the 12th-century church of **St-Sauveur**, which holds the heart of domineering warrior-knight, Bertrand du Guesclin. But there's an even better view of town and port from a stroll across the 40m (132ft) viaduct, **Vieux-Pont**, erected in 1852.

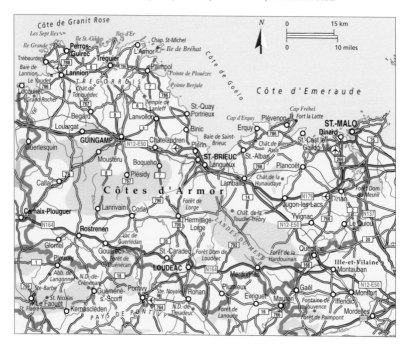

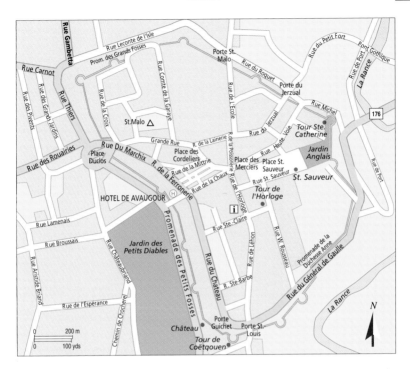

The **Château de Duchesse Anne** consists of a 14th-century castle keep and the **Tour Coëtquen** (Coëtquen tower). The keep houses a museum, while the Coëtquen tower has some interesting vaulted chambers containing a museum of stone monuments and some fine effigies.

Dinan has seen a lot of military action. When William the Conqueror besieged the town in 1065, he failed to live up to his epithet. In 1359, another attempt to capture Dinan, this time by English forces led by the Duke of Lancaster during the War of Succession, had a similar outcome: Bertrand du Guesclin held Dinan and drove the English out once and for all. There's a **statue** of Bertrand du Guesclin on horseback in the square that bears his name – it marks the exact spot where he killed Sir Thomas of Canterbury in a duel. The square is now the colourful setting for a weekly open-air market.

Bertrand du Guesclin in invincible pose in Dinan's market square.

Rue du Jerzual and **rue du Petit Fort**, the steep cobbled streets leading up to the town from the harbour, are
a feast for the eyes, but hard on the feet. Half-timbered
houses, the 16th-century homes of skilled artisans who
used to work here, have now mainly been taken over by
crêperies, but a glassblower survives.

The **tourist office** is located within the splendid 16th-
century Hôtel Kératry in rue de l'Horloge. Nearby, the
Tour de l'Horloge, a late-15th-century quadrangular
clock tower, was a gift from Duchess Anne and was used
as the Town Hall until the French Revolution. There's an
excellent view of Dinan and surrounds from the top.

If you're in town on the last weekend of September
or first weekend in October, look out for the **Fête des
Remparts**, held every even-numbered year. This is an
occasion for thousands of locals to dress in medieval costume, and there's jousting, fairs and banquets, rounded
off with a magnificent firework display.

In summer, if it is too crowded in town, walkers can
make a pleasant escape by following the rue du Jerzual,
crossing the Gothic bridge and following the towpath
upstream under the viaduct to **Léhon**, about an hour's
gentle walk away. The village has a 12th-century priory,
St-Magloire, built on the site of an abbey founded by
Nominoë. Its ruined cloisters date from the 17th century.

WEST OF DINAN

The roads inland towards **Lamballe** are particularly
interesting, as they pass through several typical Breton
villages. Lamballe itself is famous for its stud farm
(France's second most important, in business since 1825),
which produces thoroughbred horses. Guided tours are
available from 10 July until 15 September.

Southwest of Lamballe, the small fortified medieval
town of **Moncontour** is worth a detour. Built in the 11th
century, some of the town's ramparts have been preserved. Within the walls a few half-timbered and granite
houses can be seen from steep paths that connect the various levels of this hillside town. The town's church of St-
Mathurin has 16th-century stained-glass windows.

COTE D'EMERAUDE

If you head west of Dinard you enter the region of Brittany's traditional family seaside resorts, with safe beaches, picturesque towns and good camping facilities. Many places also offer excellent opportunities for sailors.

This is the **Côte d'Emeraude** (Emerald Coast), where the sea lives up to its glittering name. Even on stormy winter days when the heather-covered beaches of the **Cap Fréhel** are getting splashed with rain, the sea remains not grey, but a striking emerald-blue colour.

This is a perfect stretch of coast for sailing or walks along the cliff path, with waves lapping comfortably just below you. **St-Briac-sur-Mer**, at the mouth of the Frémur, is a particularly pretty spot, with lovely bays, sandy beaches and small offshore islands. On the second Sunday in August it hosts the Fête des Mouettes (festival of seagulls), with a procession through the town, folk dancing and a *fest-noz* night festival. Also along this coast are resorts such as **St-Lunaire**, which can boast two fine

Undoubtedly the most picturesque view of Dinan is to be had from the River Rance. Cruises depart from both St-Malo and Dinard and pass through some beautiful scenery en route.

POETIC LANDSCAPE

From Dinard to Cap Fréhel, the Côte d'Emeraude has fired the imagination of poets, writers and painters. Picasso's *Women Playing with a Ball* was inspired by Dinard in 1928.

SENTIER DES DOUANIERS

Near St-Lunaire a walk along the old 'Customs' footpath should not take more than an hour. There are good views of the Bay of St-Malo and its islets along the way. This route has inspired painters as well as the composer, Debussy. For more information, tel: 99.46.31.09.

beaches – one attractively sheltered by pines. In the town itself, an 11th-century church contains the tomb of the Irish missionary saint who gave the town its name.

Further along the coast, about 16km (10 miles) west of St-Malo, **St-Jacut-de-la-Mer** is named after a party of Irish holy men who sailed across the sea on a large lump of pumice stone in order to convert the pagan Celts. The small fishing port is now a popular family retreat, with sandy beaches, camping sites and good sailing facilities.

St-Cast-le-Guildo, with its high cliffs and seven clean beaches, is another delightful spot for a family holiday. This well-known resort, situated some 30km (20 miles) west of St-Malo, also has a picturesque fishing harbour full of pleasure boats.

Across the Bay of Sévignés from the isolated expanse of Cap Fréhel lies **Fort la Latte**, a fortress that looks ready to take on the sea in battle. The fortress, which can only be visited by guided tour, was built by corsairs and designed by Sébastien Vauban, Louis XIV's great military architect. It has two drawbridges and, inside, there is an interesting oven, built in 1795, used for heating cannon balls that were subsequently fired at the English out at sea. Guarding the approach is a menhir known as Gargantua's Finger (*le doigt du Gargantua*), looking as though it has grown naturally out of the cliffs on which it balances.

Left: *A bird's eye view of Fort la Latte, which still retains a forbidding appearance.*

Opposite: *Walks along clifftop paths afford stunning vistas.*

Past the rugged beauty of Cap Fréhel, holiday Brittany really starts, with gleaming white sands stretching seemingly forever into the distance. The evocatively named **Sables-d'Or-les-Pins** has a good stretch of golden sandy beach, situated at the foot of pine woods. This is soon put to shame by the seven excellent white-sand beaches of **Erquy**, cleansed daily by the waves. The town itself is famed for its scallops, which feature frequently on local menus. North of town, there are a number of camping sites along the promontory that leads to the Cap d'Erquy. Nearby is the charming village of **Vieux Bourg de Pléherel**, perched on a clifftop above its pine-fringed beach. The 15th-century castle moat and ramparts of **Bienassis** are situated nearby; one of the last fortified châteaux to be built in France, Bienassis was rebuilt in the 17th century and is definitely worth a visit.

At **Pléneuf-Val-André** endless vistas of empty white sands greet the eye. Here you can watch the fishing fleet come in, and the landing of scallops for later conversion to *Coquilles St-Jacques*. The rocky Pointe de Pléneuf guards the northern tip of the 2km (1^1/4-mile) sandy beach. From Pléneuf-Val-André it is possible to walk along a coastal footpath to secluded **Dahouët**, a small fishing harbour surrounded by gorse-covered cliffs.

The city of **St-Brieuc**, capital of the Côtes d'Armor and named after Brioc, one of seven saints who landed here from Britain in the 6th century, has precious little to

---

BIRDWATCHING PARADISE

Birdwatchers should head for Cap Fréhel, between Fort la Latte and Cap d'Erquy, where there are large colonies of seabirds, including fulmar, kittiwake, razorbill and herring gull, amid 300ha (741 acres) of heathland and spectacular pink sandstone cliffs; for more information, tel: 96.41.50.83.

An important winter passage place for migrating birds is at La Garde Guérin near St-Briac-sur-Mer. There are footpaths here and a good panorama of the Côte d'Emeraude as far as Cap Fréhel. For more information, tel: 99.88.32.47.

BEST BEACH

The beach of Pléneuf-Val-André is one of the best on the north coast – if not the whole of Brittany. A stroll on the promenade that leads to the Pointe de Pléneuf gives good views of St-Brieuc Bay and Erquy.

HIGH DRAMA

The cliffs along the Pointe de Plouha are the highest in Brittany, at 107m (350ft) above sea level. The Gwin Zegal footpath runs along the top and begins at the village of La Trinité.

THE CRUEL SEA

The era of the Paimpol fleet began with Louis Morand, a fearless ship-owner who was convinced he could make his fortune in Icelandic waters. With his ship *L'Occasion*, he initiated almost a century of grand adventure and prosperity. In 1895, nearly 100 ships weighed anchor and set off for the northern fisheries; many never returned from these hazardous expeditions.

BONAPARTE BEACH

Reached by a tunnel cut through the cliff, the semi-hidden Plage Bonaparte at the bottom of Cohat Bay has a fascinating history. From here, Allied pilots who had been brought down on French soil during World War II were ferried back to England, right under the noses of the German coastal patrols. A monument commemorates this astonishing act of stealth.

offer the visitor. If you do find yourself in this modern industrial city, visit the restored 14th-century **cathedral** of St-Etienne and its old district at place de la Grille.

You're much better off in **Binic**, a small fishing village that has splendid views of the sea, or the nearby resort of **Etables-sur-Mer**, with its two sandy beaches. Binic has its own museum, which details the lives of the Newfoundland fishermen who set sail from Paimpol and from all along this coast, known as the Goëlo Coast.

St-Quay-Portrieux has a number of good sandy beaches and excellent facilities for activities such as tennis and golf. There's an 18-hole course in the grounds of the 12th-century Château de Coatguelen (now a hotel), which also has riding stables and a fishing lake. Cookery courses are even held in the château's kitchens. A little further north, **Bréhec-en-Plouha** has a bay all of its own, with a beautiful sandy beach. The town is generally held to be the point where Breton begins to supplant French as the common tongue, and the further west you go from here, the more Breton-sounding the place names become.

NORTH TO PAIMPOL

You may well hear Breton spoken at the little village of **Kermaria-an-Isquit**, just inland from St-Quay-Portrieux. Its tiny **chapel**, built in yellow stone, features a sinister series of 15th-century frescoes depicting the *danse macabre* – 47 skeletal figures prancing on the wooden ceiling, led by the symbol of death himself, Ankou.

At the foot of the Paimpol peninsula, the **Abbaye Beauport** now lies mostly in ruins. Located in the middle of 40ha (99 acres) of woods and protected salt marshes, the abbey was frequently used as a stopover point for pilgrims en route for Santiago de Compostela in Galicia, northern Spain. It was built by monks in the 13th century, and later came under the direct rule of the Pope. Its abbot was allowed to wear a mitre, which elevated him to the same status as the bishop of nearby St-Brieuc. After the French Revolution, the abbey was closed and sold to raise money for the state. Only a few of its buildings remain, but its cloisters are particularly fine.

Paimpol **

Paimpol, a lively little fishing village rich in maritime history, is tinged with sadness. Reminders are everywhere of its illustrious past, when deep-sea cod-fishing fleets set sail for Iceland and Newfoundland in the 19th century. Pleasure craft and the cultivation of oysters and tourism have now replaced fishing as Paimpol's main sources of revenue, and the town remains well-to-do.

Like a fish out of water amongst pleasure craft in Paimpol's quay, *Mad Atao* is a restored Breton ketch that now serves as a floating museum dedicated to the lives of the Breton fishermen who embarked on dangerous voyages across remote seas. The port's past prosperity is also the theme of Paimpol's maritime museum, the **Musée de la Mer**, which displays models and old photographs.

The Widows' Cross (*Croix des Veuves*) at **Pors-Even** is a poignant reminder of private tragedy. Here, in days gone by, the wives of fishermen out at sea had a commanding view of the approach to Paimpol Bay as they watched for boats that were late returning to port.

A splendid stretch of sandy beach at Sables-d'Or-les-Pins near Erquy. This is a popular spot for travellers seeking a less developed Breton seaside resort.

Much has changed for the fishermen of Paimpol since the days when deep-sea fishing expeditions had to venture as far as Newfoundland to make a catch.

ON YOUR BIKES

In Paimpol you may want to spend a day cycling around the coast and inland. Bicycles can be hired from **Cycles du Vieux Clocher**, place de Verdun (open 08:30–19:30); tel: 96.20.83.58 for more details – it helps if you can speak French.

The fishermen may be gone, but they are by no means forgotten. In the rue de St-Vincent there is a chapel memorial to fishermen, and a Wall of the Deceased (*mur des disparus*) commemorates those lost at sea. And the deep-sea fishermen of Paimpol have been immortalized in print: *Le Pêcheur d'Islande* by 19th-century novelist Pierre Loti is an account of their lives.

South of Paimpol are the beautiful Romanesque ruins of the circular temple of **Lanleff**. They are of mysterious origins, but are believed to have been built by the Templars in the 11th century in the same style as the Church of the Holy Sepulchre in Jerusalem. Small figures, animals and foliage adorn the building.

A LIFE ON THE OCEAN WAVE

At Lézardrieux, near Paimpol, the Trégor sailing school is very active in organizing various sea outings on dozens of different boats – some even restored originals; for more information, tel: 96.22.87.05.

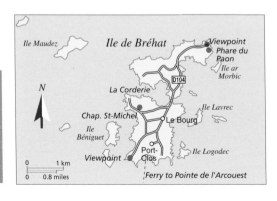

The island of Bréhat seems lost in the mists of time. Earliest recorded inhabitants were a brotherhood of monks, who set up a monastery on the island in the 5th century.

Ile de Bréhat ★★★

Paimpol makes an excellent base from which to explore the Côte de Granit Rose or to embark on a day trip to the **Ile de Bréhat**. A 10-minute ferry crossing leaves every hour in summer (every two hours off season) from the **Pointe de l'Arcouest**, 5km (3 miles) north of Paimpol.

The Ile de Bréhat is a tranquil island in which time has stood still. New construction is banned, as are cars, from its narrow, cobbled streets, making a stroll even more enjoyable. If you prefer two-wheeled locomotion, bicycles are available for rent at the ferry port.

Amid a sea bristling with reefs and islets, Bréhat is actually two islands, joined by an 18th-century **bridge**, once again designed by Sébastien Vauban. Little more than 3km (2 miles) long and 1.6km (1 mile) wide, Bréhat is a wildlife sanctuary with fig and palm trees, indicating a gentler climate than that enjoyed by the rest of the region. A network of waymarked paths adds to the pleasure of getting about the island, especially the less rugged southern part. Along the way you're likely to see mimosa and eucalyptus trees, dry-stone walls and fragrant clusters of honeysuckle.

Once home to a vibrant fishing community, the Ile de Bréhat is now a popular destination for French tourists looking for peace and quiet. Some wealthy Parisians even own second homes on the island.

Tréguier's St-Tugdual cathedral, which dates from the 14th and 15th centuries, is one of the finest examples of religious architecture in Brittany. Its stone spire laced with holes is particularly intriguing.

St Yves

Tréguier's patron saint, St Yves, is revered for his sense of fairness and for his kindness towards the poor. His spirit of justice and the speed of his judgements earned him popularity, and he frequently took on the most hopeless cases. One of Yves' most famous sayings is 'Give a poor man the benefit of the doubt'.

Maison de Renan

The 16th-century house where Ernest Renan (1823–92) was born contains memorabilia relating to the writer's life and work. Along with manuscripts and personal belongings, visitors can see an audio-visual presentation and the two small rooms at the top of the house in which Renan used to shut himself away to write.

Tréguier **

The unlikely sight of lawyers going down on their hands and knees is an annual event in Tréguier. Every year on 19 May there is a *pardon* celebrating St Yves, the patron saint of lawyers, whose tomb is located in Tréguier's stone-spired **cathedral**, one of the most overlooked in Brittany. Look closely at the Gothic spire – the perforations you can see are to protect it against the wind.

Unlike many Breton saints, about whose lives little is known beyond the layers of myth, St Yves' history is quite well documented. He was a 13th-century advocate and chaplain to the bishop of Rennes who was renowned for his incorruptibility. A friend of the poor and disadvantaged, he is believed to have died in around 1303. The *pardon* is attended by lawyers from all over the world. They proceed to **Minihy-Tréguier** a short distance south, and here crawl on their knees before a 13th-century monument in the cemetery of the church in which St Yves was born.

The French Revolution destroyed the cathedral's original stained-glass windows, as well as the tombs of St Yves and Duke Jean V, who was buried next to him. The tombs you see today are 19th-century reconstructions. Worth visiting are the cathedral's Bell Tower, the Duke's Chapel and some interesting cloisters.

Tréguier is also the birthplace, in 1823, of agnostic philosopher and historian Ernest Renan. In the main square, the place du Martray, there is a **statue** of him looking worn out after his life's work outraging the church with his theories. At his birthplace just off the square there is a small **museum** dedicated to his life.

You don't have to be a lawyer to get the most out of this pretty town on the Jaudy river, with its fine medieval houses made from stone, slate, mortar and beam. You'll need a rest after the steep climb from the port, through its old gates to the town market square, but delightful half-timbered houses en route lessen the pain immensely. Tréguier's river port is now largely used for pleasure craft, and cruises and fishing trips of this fascinating harbour town are always available in summer. Former cottages bought by English and French families as second homes are a sign of the times.

CÔTE DE GRANIT ROSE

Back on the coast, holiday Brittany continues and, at times, it can seem as though you're seeing life through rose-tinted glasses. This is the **Côte de Granit Rose** (Pink Granite Coast), approximately 20km (12¹/₂ miles) of coastline that enjoys an excellent reputation for good beaches, picturesque coves and romantic islets.

The name given to this particular stretch of coastline between Perros-Guirec and Trébeurden is easy to understand: at times the rocks seem to glow with a rich roseate

> **SEVEN ISLANDS**
>
> Nature enthusiasts are in for a treat at the offshore islands of **Les Sept-Îles**, a nature reserve and a veritable paradise for birdwatchers. Boat company **Les Vedettes Blanches** (tel: 96.23.22.47) operates daily trips in summer from Trestraou beach in Perros-Guirec.

There are a number of fine sandy beaches to choose from along the Pink Granite Coast. Perros-Guirec is a highly regarded seaside resort, with two sheltered beaches that are perfect for bathing.

Cliffs overlooking the little fishing port of Ploumanac'h are splashed yellow and purple with gorse and heather, while the pink granite boulders resemble modern sculptures.

intensity that gives them a romantic air. The colour is derived from a particular type of the mineral feldspar, which is a component of granite along with mica and quartz. The best time to appreciate the effect is at the end of a warm summer's day, when the setting sun's rays are reflected back in a blaze of salmon-pink and orange light.

Another characteristic feature of the granite along this coast is that it weathers into dramatic forms. The feldspar turns into china clay, which is washed away by water, and cracks in the coarse-grained rock have been penetrated by the sea, which over the course of centuries has eroded the quartz to sand. Wind and rain have also helped to shape the stones, and local imagination has transformed these tottering boulders into identifiable figures: the Rabbit, the Tortoise, the Pile of Pancakes.

Particularly attractive are **Plougrescant** and **Port Blanc**, a pretty old port with stone villas looking onto a sandy beach. Legend has it that in the bay of Port Blanc elves known as *korrigans* have been seen dancing on the protruding rocks, and that Morgane le Fay herself sometimes shows up in the form of a gigantic whale.

Perros-Guirec is an attractive port and resort, surrounded by the beaches of Trestraoul and Trestignel, with a harbour packed with yachts. It caters well for holiday makers: the beaches are sandy and the water's safe

BRETON TALES

Do you believe in magic? It will help if you do as legends and fairy tales grip the Breton soul. Many believe that in the bay of Port Blanc on the Côte de Granit Rose, elves or *korrigans* have been spotted dancing on the rocks offshore. But look out, evil this way comes – Ankou, the grim reaper with his tumbrel, prowls the whole peninsula, transporting souls between here, now and eternity. Beware, too, of the washwomen of the night; if you're out late, they will try to trick you into helping to wring out the burial sheets they wash at the country *lavoirs*, and will twist all your bones as they wind the sheets, unless you twist the opposite way.

for windsurfing. If you tire of sports and leisure, visit the 15th-century chapel of Notre-Dame-de-la-Clarté, a pretty pink granite building 3km (2 miles) from town.

From Perros-Guirec you can follow the old **Sentier des Douaniers** (customs path), once used to patrol the coast against smugglers, along the clifftops past weirdly shaped rock formations as far as the popular holiday resort of **Ploumanac'h**, where the pink granite rocks so evident along this coast come to the fore. Here nature has placed them one on top of the other, so delicately balanced that it's almost as if an arriving seabird will tip the scales. At the equally popular resort of **Trégastel-Plage**, huge pink-coloured rocks can be seen towering over the beach, weathered into an endless variety of shapes.

At the resort of **Pleumeur-Bodou**, which excels in sports and leisure facilities, look out for the massive golf ball (it's actually a telecommunications aerial). Ironically, there *is* a golf course nearby – the 18-hole St-Sansom course. The Côte de Granit Rose ends at **Trébeurden**, on the western tip of the Lannion peninsula. Not far away the beach resort of **St-Michel-en-Grève** and its 2km (1¹/4-mile) beach is seaside Brittany at its most enticing.

*The 'house in the chasm' (*maison du gouffre) *near Plougrescant is wedged tightly between two enormous fissured boulders.*

THALASSOTHERAPY

Like many resorts in Brittany, Perros-Guirec is a centre for thalassotherapy, the French health treatment of medical problems by the application of seawater and seaweed. It's a bit more complicated than going for a swim; you are immersed in a mixture of seaweed, mud and fresh seawater for a couple of hours every day. There are thalassotherapy institutes all over Brittany.

Guingamp's town hall dates from the late 17th century. The building was formerly an Augustinian monastery, and a section of the interior can be visited.

INLAND COTES D'ARMOR

On the banks of the River Trieux, the town of **Guingamp** west of St-Brieuc is an old weaving centre that still retains sections of its medieval ramparts. It makes a good base for exploring the nearby woodlands of Malaunay, Coat Liou and d'Avaugour, studded with megaliths, calvaries and quiet villages. In Guingamp itself notice the interesting 13th-century basilica of Notre-Dame-de-Bon-Secours, which contains a Black Virgin thought to have been brought to France by soldiers returning from the Crusades. An annual *pardon* attracts crowds of pilgrims, who join together in a torchlit procession.

Further west is **Menez-Bré**, the highest point in north Brittany at 300m (1083ft), with good views of the Monts d'Arrée and the surrounding area. At the summit is the tiny **St-Hervé** chapel, named after a blind 6th-century monk who climbed barefoot to the top. According to legend St Hervé was called upon to advise bishops who were meeting at the chapel. On his arrival, a bishop, mistaking St Hervé for a tramp, began to mock him and immediately became blind. St Hervé found water and splashed it in the bishop's eyes, thereby restoring his sight.

Lac de Guerlédan

South of St-Brieuc, the streets of the charming, quiet country town of **Quintin** are still lined with 16th-century half-timbered houses. The town was once renowned for its exquisite linen. Further south, the central closed section of the Nantes–Brest canal ends at **Lac de Guerlédan**. Surrounded by forests and fed by fast rivers burrowing into deep gorges, Lac de Guerlédan is a reservoir on the upper reaches of the Blavet river. Some quiet towns and villages nearby provide comfortable places to stay. The reservoir offers ample opportunity for a wide range of sports and activities, including sailing, fishing, windsurfing or trekking around its perimeter.

The area is also criss-crossed by a labyrinth of long-distance hiking trails, narrow lanes and waymarked circuits for ramblers, cyclists and horse-riders. Within the lake's environs are a number of attractive hamlets, including **Les Forges des Salles**, nestling at the bottom of a wooded valley. This was once an important iron-ore processing centre in the 18th and 19th centuries; the collection of workers' homes and other buildings that stand here has not been altered since 1880.

The ruins of a 12th-century Cistercian abbey provide an impressive architectural contrast to the quaintly picturesque hamlet of Les Forges. **Bon-Repos Abbey** was originally built to a very grand scale, but most of the buildings were destroyed during the French Revolution.

Côte du Guélo
Menez-Bré ▲ ● Guingamp
St-Brieuc
Lac de Guerlédan ●

GUERLEDAN BOAT TRIPS

One of the best ways to appreciate this magnificent expanse of water at the heart of the Breton *Argoat* is to take a boat trip. Boats leave regularly throughout the summer from Beau Rivage or Anse de Sordan; alternatively, canoes and kayaks may be hired between Jul and Aug from the Rond-Point du Lac in Mur-de-Bretagne.

Pony trekking in Brittany's hinterland is just one of a number of pursuits available for activity-oriented holiday makers. The area around Lac de Guerlédan contains a vast network of hiking trails, bridle paths and signposted routes for walkers.

Côtes d'Armor at a Glance

Much, of course, depends on what you want to do. In the summer months, when the temperature is conducive to seaside holidays, the beach resorts of the Côte d'Emeraude and the Côte de Granit Rose are inevitably crowded, and it is advisable to make advance reservations during this time. If sun, sea and sand are not your principal interests, spring and autumn are good seasons for walkers, while birdwatchers intent on studying the puffins and gannets on the colony of Les Sept-Iles near Perros-Guirec would benefit from a visit in spring and summer, when the breeding colonies are teeming with birds.

There are eight **trains** daily from Rennes to Morlaix, via Lamballe, St-Brieuc and Guingamp. **Buses** run hourly from Rennes to Dinan (90 min).

Four buses run from St-Brieuc to Lannion via Guingamp. Six buses run from Lannion to Trégastel and Perros-Guirec every day. **Armor Express** buses based in Dinan go direct to Dinard, Rennes and St-Malo.

Dinan

Dinan has a good selection of hotels as well as an attractive

youth hostel, which is situated some 2km (1¼ mile) from the SNCF station in the Moulin de Méen, Vallée de la Fontaine-des-Eaux. There is also a municipal camping site just outside the western ramparts on rue Chateaubriand which is open from March to November.

Hôtel L'Harlequin, 8 rue du Quai Talard, nicely situated on the quay, with good views of the River Rance and Dinan's gothic bridge, tel: 96.39.50.30.
Hôtel du Théâtre, 2 rue Sainte-Claire, adequate accommodation for budget travellers, situated across the road from the tourist office, tel: 96.39.06.91.

Paimpol

Le Répaire de Kerroc'h, 29 Quai Morand, reasonably priced, irresistible hotel with real character and historic interest, built in 1793 as a quayside mansion by Pierre Kersaux, a corsair and influential Paimpol figure; it also has a good restaurant and is open all year, tel: 96.20.50.13, fax: 96.22.07.46.

Tréguier

Hôtel Aigue Marine, Les Quais, pleasant and well-situated hotel with 50 rooms near the port overlooking the River Jaudy, tel: 96.92.39.39.

Perros-Guirec
Grand Hôtel de Trestraou, boulevard Joseph-le-Bihan,

reasonably priced hotel with views of the sea, tel: 96.23.24.05.
Le Gulf Stream, 26 rue des Sept-Iles, small hotel with restaurant and sea views, tel: 96.23.21.86.
There's also an agreeable camping site, the **Camping du Trestraou**, which is situated right beside the beach.

Dinan

When it comes to eating out in Dinan, you really are spoilt for choice, from simple pizzerias to gourmet seafood restaurants.

Les Terrasses, 2 rue du Quai, gastronomic restaurant in a beautiful location on the waterfront, tel: 96.39.09.60.
Crêperie des Artisans, 6 rue du Petit Fort, pleasant crêperie open between April and mid-October.

Paimpol

Out of season, don't leave going out to eat too late, as many places are closed by 21:30.
Restaurant du Port, Quai Morand, specializes in seafood dishes, tel: 96.20.82.76.
Crêperie Agapanthe, Quai Duguay-Trouin, friendly crêperie with good view of the quay, tel: 96.20.42.09.

Tréguier

Tréguier has several restaurants on the quayside.
Crêperie des Halles, 16 rue

Côtes d'Armor at a Glance

Ernest Renan, attractive crêperie with intimate atmosphere, open all year round, tel: 96.92.39.15.

Le Saint-Bernard, 3 rue Marcellin-Berthelot, grilled local food is a speciality in this restaurant conveniently located near the port, tel: 96.92.20.77.

TOURS AND EXCURSIONS

Activities in and Around Paimpol

Sailing and windsurfing schools

Centre Nautique du Trieux-Coz Castell, tel: 96.20.92.80. Centre Nautique des Glénans-Quai Loti, tel: 96.22.07.66.

Horse-riding

Coat Bruc in Penhoat in Plourivo, tel: 96.55.93.16. Manège 'Univers Ponies' near the beach in Bréhec-en-Plouha, tel: 96.20.37.76.

Boat trips

Le Vieux Copain (old boat) in Paimpol, tel: 96.20.59.30. *L'Ausquerne* (old boat) in Port Blanc, tel: 96.92.00.65.

Sea-fishing

La Marie-Georgette in Plougrescant, tel: 96.92.51.03.

Trips to the **Ile de Bréhat** depart from the Pointe de l'Arcouest, 5km (3 miles) north of Paimpol. **Les Vedettes de Bréhat** run day trips to the car-free island; tel: 96.55.86.99.

Centre Ornithologique de l'Ile Grande, near Pleumeur-Bodou: the ornithological centre has a permanent

exhibition relating to the area's many bird colonies; tel: 96.91.91.40.

Planétarium, Trégor: as well as a star ceiling, the planetarium has exhibitions on astrophysics, astronomy and Breton ecology. Open mid-June to mid-September, daily 11:00–12:30 and 14:00–18:30; tel: 96.91.83.78.

Lac de Guerlédan: lunch and dinner cruises in glass-topped boats are available for 1hr 30min or 3hr; tel: 96.28.52.64.

Armoripark, Bégard, northwest of Guingamp: attractions include leisure park with giant flumes, dry bobsleigh and an ice-rink. Open daily in the afternoon, all year round; tel: 96.45.36.36.

Château de Hac: located 12km (7 miles) south of Dinan at Le Quiou, the castle has exhibits of period furniture; other interesting features include attractive Renaissance gardens and candlelit tours in winter; tel: 96.83.43.06.

Boat trips to Les Sept-Iles: trips to the offshore islands, home to a variety of seabirds, are available from the Bay of Trestraou, Perros-Guirec; tel: 96.23.22.47.

Musée des Télécommunications, Pleumeur-Bodou: this museum traces the history of telecommunications – from the first underwater telegraphic cables to telecommunications in the future. Open in high season only; tel: 96.46.63.81.

USEFUL CONTACTS

Office du Tourisme de Dinan et du Pays de Dinan, 6 rue de l'Horloge, tel: 96.39.75.40, fax: 96.39.01.64.

Office du Tourisme de Pléneuf-Val-André, rue Winston Churchill, tel: 96.72.20.55.

Syndicat d'Initiative, Mairie de Tréguier, tel: 96.92.30.19.

Office Municipal du Tourisme de Paimpol, rue Pierre Feutren, tel: 96.20.83.16.

Office du Tourisme de Perros-Guirec, 21 place de l'Hôtel de Ville, tel: 96.23.21.15.

SNCF, Dinan, tel: 96.39.22.29.

Armor Express buses, Dinan, tel: 99.50.64.17.

ILE DE BREHAT	J	F	M	A	M	J	J	A	S	O	N	D
AVERAGE TEMP. °F	44	44	46	48	52	58	62	64	62	58	50	46
AVERAGE TEMP. °C	7	7	8	9	12	14	16	17	16	14	10	8
Hours of Sun Daily	2	2	4	6	7	7	8	7	6	4	2	2
RAINFALL in	3	3	2	2	2	1	1	1	2	3	4	3
RAINFALL mm	85	70	62	45	56	40	36	36	52	69	89	84
Days of Rainfall	21	16	17	14	14	12	11	13	13	16	20	19

4
Finistère

Finistère (literally, 'Land's End' in Breton) is perhaps the most Breton of all Brittany. If you need convincing, go any night into a Celtic bar in its capital, **Quimper**; you're likely to hear impromptu sessions involving Breton bagpipes and songs about relatives lost at sea.

Finistère is a strongly Celtic region of sailors and fishermen, rich in language, traditional customs and wild beauty. The famous **Pays de Bigouden**, on the Cornouaille coast to the southwest of the medieval city of Quimper, is an area of high cliffs, pounding seas and ancient fishing ports, a fiercely independent region determined to keep its personality, beliefs and distinctive costume intact against Gallic influence.

A dramatically varied coastline is Finistère's principal attraction, from pretty seaside resorts to indented granite cliffs. Deep estuaries known as *abers* are a characteristic feature of the northwest coast, and are especially scenic at high tide. Some of the small offshore islands that dot the coastline include **Batz** and **Ouessant**.

Inland, Finistère presents a landscape of windswept heath interspersed with cultivated agricultural land, vegetable farms and apple orchards. There is little forest cover, the wooded areas being mostly confined to the Parc Naturel Régional d'Armorique to the east of the **Crozon Peninsula**.

All over Finistère, tiny hamlets of immaculately whitewashed houses cluster around ancient churches – this is the home of the parish close, Brittany's most important and enduring religious architecture.

Opposite: *Quimper's St-Corentin cathedral is an impressive Gothic structure. A statue of Gradlon, ancient king of Cornouaille, sits on horseback between its two spires.*

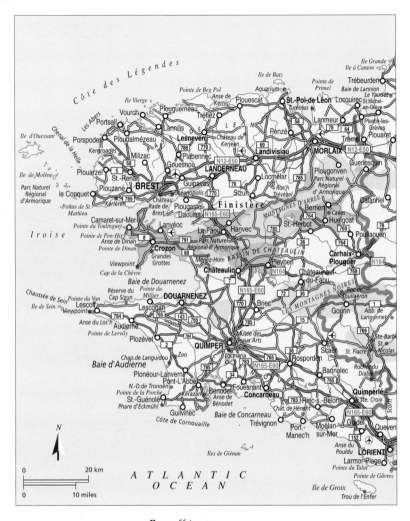

Roscoff *

Even on sunny days it looks overcast in Roscoff. This
busy ferry port is a grey town (visually, not spiritually),
made entirely of granite, and on a cloudy day it's hard to
see where the town meets the sky. Fishing and pleasure
boats are moored behind two jetties near the town centre.

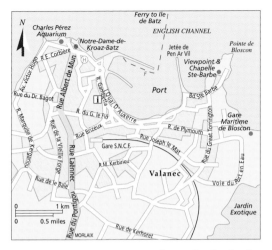

DON'T MISS

*** **Pays de Léon**: north-west Finistère's ruggedly beautiful landscape
** **Parish Close Country**: sacred architecture in the Breton heartland
*** **Crozon Peninsula**: forming part of a national park, this peninsula is one of Brittany's most appealing
** **Douarnenez**: famed sardine port, with a multitude of coloured fishing boats in Port de Rosmeur
*** **Sizun Peninsula**: Pointe du Raz, Brittany's western-most headland, affords dramatic views
*** **Locronan**: the name should be a Breton synonym for charm – some argue that this medieval town is *too* pretty
*** **Quimper**: the ancient capital of Cornouaille, with King Gradlon sandwiched between the twin spires of its cathedral.

Many visitors will leave Roscoff immediately after the ferry docks, but it's worth spending a day before moving on. The ferry port of this former smugglers' haunt is situated well out of the way of sleepy Roscoff town, which somehow always looks as though it's recovering from a hangover. The rue Gambetta is its one main street.

The peaceful tropical gardens at **Roch-Hievec**, south along the coast from the ferry terminal, have many exotic plants, including palms and cacti, which are encouraged to grow by a climate tempered by the Gulf Stream. Seawater cures can be undertaken at the **Thalassotherapy Institute**, and the Oceanology Centre is also open to visitors.

Ile de Batz

A mere 15-minute boat ride from Roscoff is the tiny **Ile de Batz** (pronounced 'baa'). Just 3km (2 miles) long and 1.6km (1 mile) wide, the island has sheltered sandy coves and an extraordinarily mild climate – only two cold days a year, so it's claimed. The island's economy is sustained by a natural resource that it has in abundance – seaweed, collected and sold for fertilizer. Perhaps this accounts for the island's popularity as a holiday destination for the region's market gardeners.

It's worth spending a day exploring the delights of old Roscoff town.

Shoppers browse among the blooms at a colourful flower market in St-Pol-de-Léon. Between January and September, the streets of this busy market town are alive with commercial traffic, bringing in supplies of local vegetables for sale at kerbside stalls.

CHATEAU DE KEROUZERE

The remains of a 15th-century granite feudal castle are situated some 8km (5 miles) to the west of St-Pol-de-Léon. Three immense corner towers survived a siege in 1590; also remaining are a stone staircase leading up to large rooms with stone window recesses, a wall walk and a guard tower. There are guided tours of the interior, which includes tapestries and a collection of 17th-century Breton furniture.

SOUTH OF ROSCOFF

Surrounded by endless fields of cabbages, artichokes and onions, in which the region excels, the nearby market town of **St-Pol-de-Léon** is situated on an attractive, curved bay full of small sailing boats. In addition to a pleasant main shopping street, the town has two interesting Gothic churches – a twin-towered 13th-century **cathedral** and the 14th- to 15th-century **Kreisker Chapel**, with a wooden barrel-vaulted roof and a fluted granite belfry that is visible for miles. A climb up all 169 steps to the top of the belfry yields splendid views over the surrounding countryside and along the coast. St-Pol-de-Léon takes its name from a Welsh monk, who crossed the Channel in the 6th century and who lived to the ripe old age of 104. The cathedral contains one of his fingers, his head and some bones from his arm.

Another finger – that of John the Baptist – gives the village of **St-Jean-du-Doigt**, 6km (10 miles) north of Morlaix, its extraordinary name. For many years its church housed what was claimed as part of the right first finger of John the Baptist. The digit was believed to have curative powers, and a new church was even built to contain it. The object of a famous annual *pardon* and pilgrimage, the finger is so precious that it is rumoured to be kept in a bank in Morlaix – in a joint account, perhaps.

Carantec and Locquirec **

Carantec is a small, attractive seaside town, custom-built for family holidays, with sandy beaches, facilities for camping, sailing, fishing and birdwatching. It is a good base for exploring the magical **Ile de Callot** at low tide, just an hour's walk away. The island's chapel contains a 16th-century statue of the Virgin, which is venerated by locals in an annual *pardon* held in August.

On the eastern edge of Finistère, where the department meets the Côtes d'Armor, the pretty little port of **Locquirec** has a walled harbour facing the Bay of Lannion. There are nine golden beaches to choose from, with dunes and gorse-covered headland. Look out for roadside stalls full of local produce from market gardens. In the town itself, there is a fine late 15th-century church.

PENN-AL-LANN PENINSULA

Just east of Carantec, the Penn-al-Lann peninsula is studded with beaches, small coves and pine forests. At the end of the peninsula there is a group of islands, the most famous of which is the Ile Louet. A footpath leads round the peninsula from Carantec's Plage du Kelenn and has wonderful views of the Trégor coast.

Low tide at Locquirec Bay leaves pleasure craft stranded. Locquirec is the most northeasterly of Finistère's seaside resorts.

Morlaix *

Heading inland, the huge arch of **Morlaix**'s magnificent
19th-century granite railway viaduct dominates this old
corsair town, with its supporting pillars soaring 60m
(200ft) above the rooftops. Lying in a deep valley, the
town's old cobbled streets and alleyways of gabled, half-
timbered houses advance northward to a yachting harbour. It is possible to look round the 16th-century house,
with its attractive Renaissance staircase and curiously
adorned wooden frontage, where Duchess Anne is said to
have stayed on a visit here in 1505. You are guaranteed a
smile when you ask locals to explain the story behind the
town's motto, 'if they bite you, bite them back [*mors-les*]'.

Morlaix's viaduct seems to announce the beginning
of a different land – some Bretons go further and claim
that it marks the barrier between the two Brittanys:
French on the one side, and Celtic heartland on the other.

Pays de Léon ***

Finistère's rugged northwestern coast is perhaps the
most dramatic in Brittany, punctuated by a series of
deep, narrow inlets known as *abers*. A few secluded
resorts dot the coastline, one of which is the former
wreckers' haunt of **Brignogan-Plage**, with good sandy
beaches and safe swimming. The family resort has a
small natural harbour, a menhir – naturally – and there
are facilities for sailing and horse-riding.

There are a number of other small, interesting ports
and tiny villages along this coast, such as **Aberwrac'h**,
Porsporder and **Portsall**, whose dubious claim to fame is
that the oil tanker *Amoco Cadiz* ran aground here in 1978,
polluting the entire coast. At **Trémazan**, the crumbling
castle is wreathed in myth: it is said to be the place
where the tragic lovers of Arthurian legend, Tristan and
Yseult, first found shelter as they fled Cornwall. The
ancient fishing village of **Le Conquet**, with its tiny harbour of old-fashioned fishing boats, is about as far west
as you can go in Brittany. It's a good base for ferry trips
to the offshore islands of Ouessant and Molène, and
there are pleasant walks along scenic coastal footpaths.

Left: *St-Mathieu was once a town of some importance in the 14th century, though today it is known only for the remains of its Benedictine abbey church and its lighthouse, which affords a panoramic view from the top.*

The land's end of this peninsula is the dramatic rocky headland of **Pointe St-Mathieu**, the most northerly of the three capes in Finistère. Excellent views of the Atlantic and its jagged offshore islands are to be had from here. A short distance to the north is the Point de Corsen, the most westerly part of continental France.

Opposite: *In an attractive waterside setting, Morlaix is compact and can easily be explored on foot, though be prepared for some stiff climbs up steep steps connecting the upper and lower parts of town.*

Ile d'Ouessant ★

A journey of some 2^1/$_2$hr by boat from Brest, Ouessant (better known as Ushant to English speakers) is a rugged yet beautiful archipelago of eight islands, where sheep outnumber the human population. It's a place where women have traditionally worn the trousers. Because their menfolk spent months away at sea, the island's women learned to farm the land and, where necessary, propose marriage instead of waiting to be asked.

The island's capital is the small port of **Lampaul**, whose church of Notre-Dame-de-Bon-Voyage contains small wax crosses that stand as poignant memorials to those lost at sea. At nearby **Niou**, you can see a reconstruction of a typical island dwelling in the Ecomusée.

Visitors to Ouessant are attracted not only by its surprisingly diverse scenery, but also by the superb birdwatching opportunities afforded along its exposed northern coast. Be sure to visit the Pointe de Pern, an area of stunning rocks. The island also enjoys a tolerably mild climate, although the atmosphere can become rather bleak when winter mists descend.

> ### THE *NAUFRAGEURS*
>
> Farmers from villages on this most rugged of Brittany's coastlines used to be so poor that they were forced to pillage the bounty of shipwrecks brought in by the sea. During bad storms these men – or *naufrageurs* (wreckers), as they came to be known – would gather on the shore and prepare to plunder. They would sometimes give fate a helping hand with lanterns tied to the horns of cattle to imitate a lighthouse and lure ships on to the rocks.

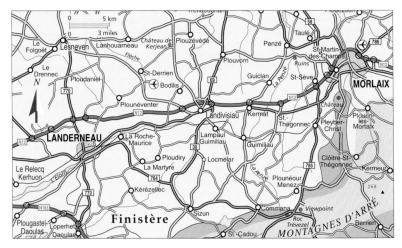

PARISH CLOSE COUNTRY ★★

Parish closes (*enclos paroissiaux*) are the most important religious monuments in Brittany, clustered mainly around the Pays de Léon and Cornouaille in the south of Finistère. They serve as a symbolic link between the spiritual community of the present and that of the dead.

A parish close is the sacred ground of a Breton community. It is enclosed by a wall and usually comprises a church and cemetery, an ossuary, or receptacle for bones, and a calvary – a granite statue depicting Biblical scenes and surmounted by a crucifixion. The most famous are to be found at St-Thégonnec, Guimiliau, Lampaul-Guimiliau, Sizun, Commana and Pleyben.

The ornate parish close at **St-Thégonnec** combines Renaissance, Baroque and Classical styles featuring many sculptures and decorative figures, including one of Christ being scourged by soldiers. The west front of the calvary has an altar that was used for open-air celebrations of Mass when the congregation became too large for the parish church.

Southwest of St-Thégonnec, the famous calvary at **Guimiliau**, dating from the 16th century, features more than 200 statues illustrating the life and passion of Christ. Look out also for the demons tearing to shreds the figure of Katell Gollet, an impious woman who made love with the Devil, stole a consecrated holy wafer for him, and was thrown into hell. The late Renaissance church at Guimiliau is adorned with a number of elaborate carvings, and is a splendid example of Breton architecture.

The oldest of all parish closes is the one situated at **Lampaul-Guimiliau**, just south of Morlaix, with its fine Renaissance funerary chapel and triumphal arch. The church's south porch has statues of the 12 Apostles.

Landivisiau is a good base for visiting the parish closes, but has little else to entice the visitor, unlike **Plougastel-Daoulas**, not far from Brest, which has a 17th-century calvary that has skilfully been restored after suffering air-raid damage in 1944. The town specializes in a liqueur made from strawberries (*fraises*). The parish close and abbey at **Daoulas**, with its Romanesque cloisters and chevet, is said to be the most beautiful in Brittany. Some 32 arches remain, decorated with Celtic motifs and expressively carved figures and foliage.

The parish close at St-Thégonnec is one of the most impressive in Brittany, and is also a much visited shrine.

Château de Kerjean *

One of the many castles and manors in this part of Finistère is situated at **St-Vougay**, just 15km (9^1/$_2$ miles) south of Roscoff. The Château de Kerjean is vaunted as the 'Versailles of Brittany', but don't be put off by such extravagant promotion. Although it has a moat, the château is in fact a very handsome 16th-century mansion that stands majestically at the end of a long avenue of trees. It now contains an exhibition of Breton furniture, including some claustrophia-inducing box-beds.

WALKING IN THE PARK

The grounds of the Château de Kerjean are dotted with Renaissance relics, including a charming fountain set into a stone wall. After the 17th and 18th centuries the gardens were designed to be used for peaceful walks.

Lesneven and Le Folgoët **

Little remains of the ramparts of the old fortified town of **Lesneven**, but a cloister attached to the Maison d'Accueil houses an interesting regional museum.

A short distance southwest of Lesneven, the stained-glass windows of **Le Folgoët's** impressive 15th-century Gothic basilica tell the story behind the town's name. In the 14th century, a simpleton named Al Fool-goat ('the fool of the wood') was reputed to live under a tree, sustaining himself by begging for food. He spent his life repeating the only two words of Latin he knew, *Ave Maria*. After his death, a white lily sprouted from his grave with the words *Ave Maria* written in gold on its petals. Later, in 1364, Duke Jean IV laid the foundation stones of the great church of Notre-Dame that now stands on the site. The church became a renowned centre of pilgrimage, and one of Brittany's most important *pardons* takes place here on the first Sunday in September.

Brest

The wild beauty synonymous with Finistère is in rather short supply in Brest. Unless you have a particular interest in the extensive use of concrete, this industrial port has little to detain the visitor.

It is fashionable to criticize the town's ugliness, the result of over-rapid reconstruction after virtual total destruction in a six-week bombardment during World War II. Today, nothing survives of ancient Brest other than its château – now the headquarters of the Préfecture Maritime – and the 15th-century **Tanguy** tower, which has a museum about the old town.

A gateway to the Crozon Peninsula, Brest's splendid natural harbour is home to the *Royale* – the French Atlantic Fleet. Even today the naval dockyard is subject to strict security, and is restricted to French nationals only. Being such a well-sheltered port, Brest has repelled attacks from Henry VIII to Hitler. Incidentally, the *Bismarck* was on its way to Brest when it was sunk.

Brest does have good facilities for nautical sports and cruising. It also stages an interesting summer festival focusing on Breton stories and legends. Also worth seeing is the massive **Océanopolis**, a scientific and technical research centre dedicated to study of the marine environment.

It is wiser to spend some time in **Landerneau**, a pretty port and lively market town on the Elorn river, which widens out to form the town's harbour. A centre of attraction in town is the 16th-century **pont de Rohan**, one of the last bridges in Europe lined with houses on both sides. In the Middle Ages, water power was used to operate the machinery in the mills. On the right bank of the river are some 17th-century turreted houses.

Former capital of the Léon region, the small market town of Landerneau is now best known for its picturesque Rohan bridge and its attractive old houses on the right bank of the Elorn river.

THE CROZON PENINSULA ★★★

The tiny medieval port of **Le Faou** stands at the entrance to one of Brittany's most attractive peninsulas, part of which forms a section of the Parc Naturel Régional d'Armorique. The summit of 330m (1082ft) **Ménez-Hom** makes a good point from which to survey the surrounding landscape, with panoramic views over the Bay of Douarnenez and the Brest estuary. A folklore festival is held on top of Ménez-Hom on 15 August every year.

Coastal view of Morgat, a sheltered seaside resort with a large sandy beach. Its harbour has room for 400 pleasure craft, and there are opportunities for all types of fishing.

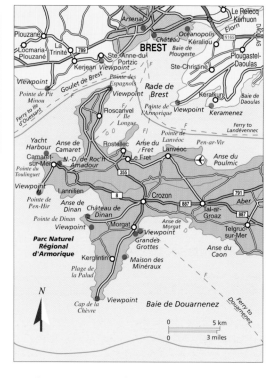

The largest town on the peninsula is **Crozon**, though it has little of interest for visitors. Nearby **Morgat** is a much better proposition, with sheltered sands and an attractive harbour bobbing with pleasure craft. Boat trips can be taken from here to visit the numerous multi-coloured *grottes* (caves) that indent the coastline, while walkers can enjoy a clifftop path that extends as far as the Cap de la Chèvre, jutting into Douarnenez Bay.

On the tip of the Crozon Peninsula is the small lobster port of **Camaret-sur-Mer**, which has a few good seafood restaurants. Nearby is the megalithic site of **Lagatjar**, which has more than 100 standing stones arranged in lines and ending in a circle. The town makes a good though expensive base from which to explore the peninsula. Another good view of the coast and offshore islands can be had from the clifftop bird sanctuary perched 68m (224ft) up on the **Pointe du Penhir**. Below, a succession of rocks protruding into the sea gives the impression of a cliff that has tried and failed to break.

Douarnenez **

Not many places can do it, but **Douarnenez** successfully manages a juggling act. It is both an exciting seaside resort and a hard-working commercial port – one of France's top fishing ports, in fact. Its name is believed to derive from the Breton *Douar Nevez* (new land), which replaced King Gradlon's lost city of Ys.

Its wide bay has some fine beaches, especially the **Plage des Dames**. There's also a sailing school, a marina and an all-year-round thalassotherapy centre in the neighbouring town of **Tréboul**. The fascinating **Port-Musée** is also situated here, on the site of Port-Rhu.

> **PORT-MUSEE**
>
> Located below Douarnenez's bridge is the **Port-Musée** (tel: 98.92.65.20), which contains a large and varied collection of fishing boats moored for visitors to board and explore. On the quay, displays and workshops demonstrate the traditional work of the local fishermen and oyster farmers.

Douarnenez's chief attraction is its pretty setting. Colourful quaysides and old streets full of character add to its charm. Despite its tranquil exterior, the town's port is one of Brittany's busiest.

THE DROWNED CITY OF YS

Ys was the ancient city of Gradlon, King of Cornouaille, and is now believed to lie beneath the waves in Douarnenez Bay. Gradlon built the city behind dikes for his daughter, Dahut. But she was seduced by the Devil, who ordered her to steal the keys to the floodgates from her father as he slept. During high tide the Devil unlocked the gates and the city was submerged beneath the waves. The king escaped, pushing his daughter into the waves as she attempted to cling to his horse. Debussy's piano prelude, *La Cathédrale Engloutie*, was inspired by the legend. Even today some fishermen have reported hearing the church bells of the lost city ringing beneath the water.

CRIEES

In the fishing towns of Douarnenez and Concarneau, look out for the early morning *criée* – a colourful Breton fish auction. The auctions start when tunny fish, lobster and crab are unloaded and bidding begins. In Concarneau, check out the Quai Carnot between 06:30 and 11:00, or follow your nose around the Rosmeur port area of Douarnenez.

Follow your nose down to the harbour area of **Port du Rosmeur**, which, on a sunny day, is as colourful a spot as you're likely to find in all Brittany. The best known *pardon* in the whole of the region takes place every year at **Ste-Anne-la-Palud**, on the edge of the Bay of Douarnenez, at the end of August. Thousands gather at the town's 19th-century chapel, which contains a painted granite statue of St Anne, and high Mass is celebrated, followed by a procession.

A Fishy Business

By the end of the 19th century, Douarnenez was the biggest sardine port in Europe, with 32 canneries. With ubiquitous drying nets, net repairers, can makers, canneries and boatyards, the town lived and breathed sardines, and the number of canning factories continued to grow until 1940. However, by the 1960s, a sea change in fishing techniques meant that the Breton sardine was too large for conventional tinning, and fish had to be brought in from the Mediterranean or Atlantic. Today only three canneries remain in Douarnenez, although it is still the European leader in tinned sea products, with an annual turnover of 25,000 tons of fish, scallops and crustaceans. One survivor still producing is the famous Chancerelle family, founded in 1853, which trades under the brand name of Connétable. It favours its production of sardines *à l'ancienne*, a specification that guarantees that the fish are prepared according to time-honoured methods of frying in olive or peanut oil.

THE SIZUN PENINSULA ***

The long promontory to the west of Douarnenez is known as the Sizun Peninsula, which ends at the **Baie des Trépassés** (Bay of the Dead). The bay is named after the sailors who were drowned in numerous shipwrecks along this coast. Their bodies were ferried by priests across the bay to their final resting place on the Ile de Sein. Legend has it that on 2 November every year, all the souls of those drowned in the Baie des Trépassés come together in search of their loved ones.

The splintered granite cliffs of the Pointe du Raz form a diminishing chain of reefs that reaches far into the sea. On the last of these rocky promontories perches the Veille lighthouse.

The peninsula ends dramatically at the awe-inspiring serrated cliffs of the **Pointe du Raz**, the westernmost point of Brittany (and France), and the most southerly of Finistère's three headlands. If cameras are clashing with those of fellow visitors (it can be very busy here), try the **Pointe du Van** further north. Admittedly it's not as dramatic, but it is hardly ever crowded.

Ile de Sein

Just offshore lies the Ile de Sein. There is plenty of birdlife on this tiny, flat island, which barely rises 1.5m (5ft) above sea level. In the past its inhabitants have had to take refuge on the rooftops. The island's moment of glory came in June 1940, when General de Gaulle delivered his appeal for volunteers to join the Free French forces. Every man and boy of fighting age from the island sailed to England to help. Their enthusiasm was rewarded after the war when de Gaulle made a visit to award the inhabitants with a Liberation Cross.

SEABIRDS-R-US

On the north-facing coast of the Sizun Peninsula, the Cap Sizun bird sanctuary is home to numerous species of seabirds, including puffins, fulmars, razorbills and herring gulls, all in their natural element and not prepared for the camera. The sanctuary (tel: 98.70.13.53) is open daily from Mar to the end of Aug, 10:00–12:00, 14:00–16:00.

*Hanging flower baskets add
a dash of colour to a
medieval house in
Locronan.*

Locronan ✭✭✭

A visit to **Locronan**, some 10km (6 miles)
inland from Douarnenez, is like being
transported back into the Middle Ages.
Medieval buildings, a beautiful cobbled
square surrounded by fine Renaissance
houses and an ancient well in the centre,
have all earned the town its reputation as
the most picturesque in Brittany. It has a
15th-century church with old statues and attractive stone
vaulting. The chapel contains the cenotaph of the Irish
Saint Ronan, from whom Locronan takes its name. He
preached and was buried here in the 5th century, and
there is a *pardon* in his honour every July. The town used
to earn its living by making sailcloths for the French
navy, but tourism is now the main source of livelihood.
Locronan's local history museum is located up the hill in
the Conservatoire de l'Affiche. On clear days there are
good views of the town and surrounding countryside.

Pays de Bigouden ✭✭

Between the Ile de Sein and Plozévet, the lobster and
crayfish port of **Audierne**, with its long stretch of sandy
shore and exceptionally clean water, marks the start of
the Pays de Bigouden. On market mornings in certain
towns, it is sometimes still possible to see women wear-
ing their unusually tall white-lace *coiffes*.

At the end of this coast is the **Pointe de Penmarch**,
which has the immense Eckmühl lighthouse at its southernmost point, and the 15th-century Notre-Dame-de-la-
Joie chapel, both open to visitors. The nearby calvary of
Notre-Dame-de-Tronoën, believed to be the oldest of all
the great Breton calvaries, relates the story of Christ.

Past the small, charming town of **Le Guilvinec**,
renowned for its sardines, **Pont-l'Abbé** is the capital of
the Pays de Bigouden. It has a display of traditional costumes and lace *coiffes* at its folklore museum, the Musée
du Bigouden, located in a 14th-century castle keep. Quite
by contrast, expert windsurfers who know their stuff
head for the **Pointe de la Torche** east of St-Guénolé.

Quimper ✶✶✶

This most Breton of cities in its pretty valley setting takes its name from a French corruption of the Breton word *kemper*, meaning a confluence of rivers. In Quimper's case, it is three rivers: the Steir, the Jet and the Odet, which flows through the city centre.

Quimper is the erstwhile capital of Cornouaille, a duchy of medieval Brittany that extended from Morlaix in the north as far as Quimperlé to the east. The city's heart lies in its seductive cobbled streets, untouched by World War II bombing – Quimper was thought to be of too little strategic importance.

The twin spires of its Gothic **cathedral** frame a statue of the legendary 6th-century King Gradlon. The cathedral was built between the 13th and 15th centuries, although the spires were not added until the 19th. Dedicated to St Corentin, the first bishop of Quimper, the cathedral has vast 15th-century stained-glass windows and is probably best visited during a Breton-language service. Right next door to the cathedral is the **Musée Départemental Breton** (closed Tuesday), which specializes in pottery, artefacts and Breton country costume.

Inside the 65m (213ft) Eckmühl lighthouse, perched at the end of the Pointe de Penmarch, a staircase spirals upwards to the viewing gallery, from where there is a panoramic view along the coast.

PAYS DE BIGOUDEN

The Bigouden region takes its name from the tall lace *coiffes* worn by Bigoudène women (from *begou*, point; *den*, person). There have been many nicknames for these headdresses over the years, including sugar loaves and Eckmühl lighthouses (after the huge lighthouse that stands at the very tip of the Pointe de Penmarch).

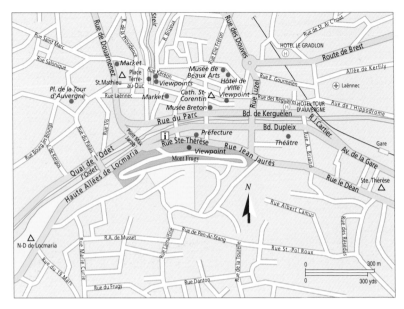

There's an excellent view of the medieval city from 87m (285ft) **Mont Frugy** across the river. Afterwards you'll have earned some refreshment at the L'Eppé bar just opposite. Waiters once used to pay for the privilege of working here because they could earn so much in tips.

The **pont Max Jacob**, Quimper's main bridge across the Odet, is named after a Jewish writer who converted to Catholicism. He was, however, still forced to wear a yellow star during the Nazi occupation, and died en route for the gas chambers.

Quimper specializes in pottery and earthenware (*faïence*). Traditional designs painted on a pale blue glaze feature Breton peasants at work and play, and can be found all over Quimper at street markets.

The largest celebration of Breton culture takes place at Quimper's **Fête de la Cornouaille**, which is held in the second half of July. The action involves concerts, street musicians and traditional costume parades, and the festival has become an international event, attracting interest the world over.

STREET ENTERTAINMENT

Walking around the streets of Quimper is rarely a dull affair, as there is usually something musical going on. Keep a look out for musical accompaniment in the form of travelling musicians and lute players, or street entertainers such as trapeze artists, mime acts and fire eaters. And don't leave Quimper without seeing the twin spires of its cathedral lit up at night.

FINISTERE'S SOUTH COAST

Loctudy, 6km (4 miles) to the south of Pont-l'Abbé, is a tiny fishing port and seaside resort with fine beaches and sand dunes. Boat services run from here to Quimper and the **Iles des Glénans**, an archipelago of islets that boasts a variety of birdlife, dreamy lagoons and deserted white sandy beaches. Boats also run from **Bénodet**, a popular, purpose-built resort situated on the Odet estuary. An upmarket yachting centre with a marina, it can get very busy here during high season, when people come to show off their boats.

To the east, **Fouesnant** is surrounded by apple and cherry orchards. Its strong, locally produced cider is regarded as Brittany's finest. If you need to clear your head after sampling some, Fouesnant also has good, safe beaches and wooded sand dunes. Nearby **Beg-Meil**, a former fishing village with coves, is fringed by white sand and pines. The town still functions as a lobster port, despite the many pleasure craft that give it the appearance of hosting a boat show.

Boats on parade at Bénodet's chic marina.

Concarneau ✱

Concarneau is an ancient fishing town, still intact behind 15th-century fortifications anchored alongside an ugly, modern town with high-rise housing. Today it is a big tuna-fishing port. The old walled town of **Ville Close**, on a narrow island in the middle of the harbour, is similar to Mont-St-Michel, without the tiring uphill walks. Narrow cobbled streets are full of shops to attract tourists, but there are some signs of local life, such as the colourful open market. The early-morning fish auctions (*criées*), held at about 07:30 on Quai Carnot, are worth investigation for an insight into Breton character.

CANNING TOWN

Concarneau is a port renowned for its sardines. The earliest sardine cans ever made can be seen in the town's fishing museum, **Musée de la Pêche** (tel: 98.97.06.59), in rue Vauban. But tinning sardines did not seal the town's prosperity – this came more through its discovery of medieval treasure – and tuna fishing is Concarneau's biggest money spinner today.

Opposite: *On the western edge of the Montagnes Noires stands Ménez-Hom, at 330m (1083ft) the highest peak in Brittany.*

Below: *Gauguin's work of the Pont-Aven period shows typically Breton themes. The Pont-Aven School of painting is characterized by its use of vivid colours and two-dimensional forms.*

Pont-Aven **

The river port of **Pont-Aven** owes its fame to an expressionist school of painters, formed by Paul Gauguin in 1888, who were captivated by the charm of Cornouaille, in Brittany's southwest corner.

Beside the bridge, the **Hôtel Ajoncs d'Or** (whose name means 'golden gorse') is the *pension* where Gauguin stayed, now a newsagent/bookshop. But ancient watermills on the banks of the Aven still survive, and there is an attractive walk along the river banks, with views of the harbour and its pleasure boats.

To see what inspired Gauguin and other artists, stroll above the river through the **Bois d'Amour** (walking maps are available). A museum in the town hall at place de l'Hôtel-de-Ville has a selection of paintings from the Pont-Aven school. The tourist office is also located here.

Visitors can follow in the footsteps of Paul Gauguin and the Pont-Aven school of painters, visiting the places depicted in their paintings of Breton peasants and fishermen, and the villages and countryside in which they lived. The **Route des Peintres en Cornouaille** goes to Trémalo, Nizon Le Hénan, Kerascoët, Bélon harbour and Le Pouldu, where Gauguin later moved when Pont-Aven became too crowded. While the focus is most definitely on painting, the tour also takes in a mixture of local architecture and gastronomic specialities. The staff at Pont-Aven's tourist office can supply details.

Quimperlé **

Quimperlé is an attractive town on two levels connected by flights of steps at the junction of the Ellé and Isole rivers. Seek out the circular **Eglise Ste-Croix**, surrounded by medieval houses, and the Louis XIV Chapel of the Convent of **Notre-Dame-de-l'Assomption** (nicknamed the 'sugar loaf'). Quimperlé has good crêperies and restaurants,

and specializes particularly in seafood and oysters from nearby Riec sur Bélon, as well as some very drinkable local ciders. The nearby coastal fishing villages of **Moëlan**, **Doëlan** and **Le Pouldu**.

CENTRAL FINISTERE **

In the heart of Finistère stand the **Monts d'Arrée**, reaching no more than 300m (1083ft) at their highest point, though they seem like mountains compared with the surrounding moorland. They form part of the Parc Naturel Régional d'Armorique, a vast conservation area that was set up in 1969 to protect the wildlife and ancient megalithic sites of western Brittany.

On the southern edge of the Monts d'Arrée, the small village of **Huelgoat** on the Argent river is a good base for walkers and fishing enthusiasts. It has a few hotels and its own small lake, situated next to woods and valleys that are ideal for exploring. Littering the ground are magnificent wind-sculpted rocks, some of which have been eroded into evocative shapes.

If the Monts d'Arrée are central Finistère's heart, the **Montagnes Noires** are its spine. This range of rolling hills is where myth and mystique are inseparably entwined with heathlands of gorse and broom, jagged crests and rocks, peatbeds, trout streams, forests, woodlands, fenland green and wooded valleys. The name, Black Mountains, suggests that this area was once extensively forested, although little sign now remains.

NATURE WALKS

The Parc Naturel Régional d'Armorique extends for more than 95,000ha (234,742 acres) over the Crozon Peninsula and on to the uplands of the Monts d'Arrée. Deer and wild boar roam in the woods of **Ménez-Meur** and **Hanvec**, and beavers run free at **Brennelis** and **Loqueffret**.

THE LEGEND OF HOK-BRAS

There's virtually a legend behind every story in Brittany, and the Monts d'Arrée are no exception. Long ago, a gentle giant named Hok-Bras lived between Landerneau and Daoulas; when he was bored, he would toss pebbles into the vale. It is believed that this is why the forest of Huelgoat contains so many heavy blocks of granite. Hok-Bras is also said to be responsible for the creation of the Monts d'Arrée – his excuse was that he was just a normal child who liked to pile up sand and pebbles.

Finistère at a Glance

As elsewhere in Brittany, a compromise has to be made between summer crowds and off-season closures. Places such as the dramatic Pointe du Raz and Locronan are seething with visitors in July and August especially. If beach holidays are your main interest, temperatures along Finistère's more exposed northern coast can be cooler outside the summer months than the more sheltered south coast resorts of Concarneau, Beg-Meil and Bénodet. You may also want to time your visit to coincide with one of the many *pardons* held throughout the department between May and September. Concarneau's annual event is the **Fête des Filets Bleus** (Blue Nets Festival), held on the third Sunday in August.

GETTING THERE

Brittany Ferries operates a year-round **ferry crossing** from Plymouth to Roscoff (6hr) or from Cork to Roscoff (19hr). Fares vary according to season. For more information, tel: 01752 221321.

Brit Air operates seasonal **flights** to Quimper. **Trains** run from Paris to Brest, via Landerneau, Landivisiau, Morlaix and Rennes.

GETTING AROUND

Six **trains** a day run from Brest to Quimper (journey time: 90 min). There are **buses** from Brest to Roscoff, via Lesneven and Lanhouarneau. Five buses a day operate between Quimper to Locronan (journey time: 25 min); for details of services, tel: 98.90.50.50.

WHERE TO STAY

Roscoff
Hôtel Bellevue, boulevard Jeanne d'Arc, friendly hotel and restaurant with good view of the harbour, open mid-March until mid-November, tel: 98.61.23.38.
Hôtel Thalassatonic, avenue Victor Hugo, tel: 98.29.20.20.

Landerneau
Le Clos du Pontic, rue du Pontic, good hotel and restaurant that enjoys an excellent reputation for local seafood dishes; it also makes a good base for exploring parish closes, tel: 98.21.50.91, fax: 98.21.34.33.

Brest
Hôtel des Voyageurs, 15 avenue Clemenceau, well-located hotel and restaurant in the heart of the city, tel: 98.80.25.73.

Douarnenez
Hôtel La Bretagne, 23 rue Duguay-Trouin, pleasant hotel, near the tourist office and en route for the Port du Rosmeur, no restaurant, tel: 98.92.30.44.

Locronan
Du Prieuré, reasonably priced small hotel on the road to main cobbled square; it's advisable to book in advance, tel: 98.91.70.89.

Quimper
Hôtel Gradlon, 30 rue de Brest, charming, three-star hotel run by friendly Anglo-French couple; the bed in its showpiece room once belonged to artist Paul Sérusier, a Gauguin contemporary, tel: 98.95.04.39, fax: 98.95.61.25.
Hôtel Dupleix, 34 boulevard Dupleix, well-positioned modern hotel near the Max Jacob bridge, tel: 98.90.53.35, fax: 98.52.05.31.

WHERE TO EAT

Roscoff
Chardons Bleus, 4 rue de l'Amiral Réveillère, specializes in seafood, tel: 98.69.72.03.

Landerneau
Au Feu de Bois, 16 rue des Boucheries, good restaurant and crêperie, specializing in Portuguese cuisine, very popular with local clientele, tel: 98.21.46.31.
La Mairie, 9 rue de la Tour d'Auvergne, seafood is a speciality at this restaurant near the Rohan bridge, tel: 98.85.01.83.

Douarnenez
Le Mascaret, 54 rue Duguay-Trouin, speciality is seafood, especially *Coquilles St-Jacques au beurre blanc* (scallops in a mouthwatering butter sauce), tel: 98.92.84.34.

Finistère at a Glance

Au Goûter Breton, 36 rue Jean Jaurès, an excellent place to sample traditional Breton crêpes, tel: 98.92.02.74.

Locronan
La Pierre de Lune, place des Charrettes, restaurant and crêperie specializing in grilled meat dishes, tel: 98.91.82.20.

Quimper
Le Capuchin Gourmand, 29 rue des Réguaires, good regional and traditional cooking, tel: 98.95.43.12.
La Rive Gauche, 9 rue Sainte-Catherine, good value-for-money restaurant; everything is freshly prepared, and the meat dishes are especially good, tel: 98.90.06.15.

Concarneau
Le Galion, 15 rue St-Guénolé, the house speciality is *cotriade* (fish stew); there is also a hotel attached that has a small number of rooms; it's advisable to book in advance, tel: 98.97.30.16.

Pont-Aven
Moulin de Rosmadec, well situated on a terrace on the river, expensive but excellent fish dishes.

TOURS AND EXCURSIONS

Quimper is understandably keen to show off its rich heritage, and this is made easier with a **Passeport culturel** (available between 4 May and 15 Oct). The ticket allows entry to all of Quimper's top

museums, including the Musée Départemental Breton, Musée des Beaux-Arts, the famous china factory of Faïencerie HB-Henriot, Musée de la Faïence (museum of pottery and ceramic art), and the Centre d'Art Contemporain. An authorized tour of Quimper is also part of the deal. The pass costs between FF50 and FF100 and is available from Quimper's Office du Tourisme.
Musée d'Art et Nature: set in an old farm in the Monts d'Arrée, in the village of Kervelly near Commana, the museum features an underground view of a fox's den, a Roe deer's passage and a gardenful of wildlife such as peacocks, pheasants and badgers. Open in season between 10:00 and 18:00; tel: 98.78.03.43.
Musée du Cidre: the Brittany Cider Museum at the Vergers de Kermarzin, in Argol, central Finistère, has the best exhibition in France dedicated to apples and cider. Tours and tastings prove popular; tel: 98.27.73.26.
Château de Trévarez: near Châteauneuf de Faou, the

castle has stables, fountains and a pool in an 85ha (210-acre) setting of wooded grounds; tel: 98.26.82.79.
Tours of sea caves: at Morgat on the Crozon Peninsula, tours operate daily between May and September, depending on weather; tel: 98.27.09.54.
Pyramid Lighthouse: at Bénodet, open daily between mid-March and October; tel: 98.57.24.77.

USEFUL CONTACTS

Office du Tourisme de Roscoff, 46 rue Gambetta, tel: 98.61.12.13, fax: 98.69.75.75.
Office du Tourisme de Quimper, place de la Résistance, tel: 98.53.04.05, fax: 98.53.31.33.
Office du Tourisme de Plougastel-Daoulas, 4 place du Calvaire, 29470 Plougastel-Daoulas, tel: 98.40.34.98.
Office du Tourisme de Concarneau, Quai d'Aiguillon, tel: 98.97.01.44.
Office du Tourisme de Douarnenez, tel: 98.92.13.35, fax: 98.74.46.09.

BREST	J	F	M	A	M	J	J	A	S	O	N	D
AVERAGE TEMP. °F	42	42	46	48	54	58	62	62	60	54	48	44
AVERAGE TEMP. °C	6	6	8	9	12	14	16	16	15	12	9	7
Hours of Sun Daily	2	3	4	6	7	7	8	7	6	4	3	2
RAINFALL in	5	4	4	3	3	2	2	2	3	4	5	6
RAINFALL mm	138	102	105	72	76	55	46	59	80	110	121	140
Days of Rainfall	22	19	20	17	16	14	13	15	15	18	21	21

5
Morbihan and Nantes

Morbihan (Breton for 'little sea') is named after the Golfe de Morbihan, and is ironically the only one of Brittany's four *départements* with a Breton name.

The Golfe de Morbihan is essentially an estuary south of the port of **Vannes**, its medieval capital. The exact number of islands scattered in the Gulf is still a mystery, ranging between 43 and 365. It has strong Gallo-Roman associations, too, since it was here that Julius Caesar saw his last Breton enemies, the Veneti, defeated in 56BC.

Today, enemies have long since departed, replaced by a friendly climate of sandy beaches, charming fishing villages, medieval towns and sheltered harbours. The exotic offshore islands of **Ile de Groix**, accessible from the busy port of **Lorient**, and **Belle-Ile**, reached by boat from **Quiberon**, are popular holiday destinations.

Thanks to the warming effect of the Gulf Stream, Morbihan's climate is so mild and its vegetation so lush that you can be forgiven for occasionally thinking yourself on the shores of the Mediterranean rather than the Atlantic. The sophisticated beach resort of **La Baule** further compounds the impression, with its row upon row of sun-baked bodies, expensive shops and designer beachwear. To escape the crowds, the nearby resorts of **Pornichet** and **Le Croisic** are attractive alternatives.

Just when you think you've got to know Morbihan, there's the little matter of stones – the alignments of prehistoric megaliths at **Carnac**, which continue to puzzle experts today. Theories abound – some plausible, others frankly bizarre; myth and magic still exercise their grip.

MORBIHAN CLIMATE

Morbihan's luxuriant green vegetation testifies to the fact that it enjoys a settled climate, with consistently warm temperatures between June and mid-October. Winters are mild, and it seldom snows.

Opposite: *Port-Navalo is a peaceful port and seaside resort on the tip of the Rhuys Peninsula, with good views over the Golfe de Morbihan.*

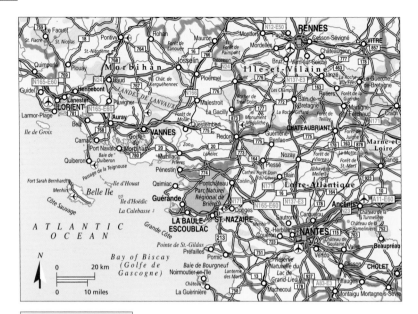

DON'T MISS

** **Josselin**: hillside town on the River Oust with a stunning medieval castle
** **Rochefort-en-Terre**: a picturesque medieval village
*** **Belle-Ile**: romantic and remote – the largest of Brittany's offshore islands
*** **Carnac**: thousands of mysterious standing stones that have baffled generations
** **St-Goustan**: the old port of Auray, with its medieval bridge, half-timbered houses and cobbled streets
** **Vannes**: fortified gateway to the Golfe de Morbihan
** **La Baule**: a slice of the Mediterranean in Brittany's most sought-after resort
** **Nantes**: ancient former capital of Brittany rich in historical associations.

Lorient

Like Brest, **Lorient** was virtually destroyed during its liberation in 1944. Today, it is a submarine base and commercial port, currently the second largest in France. It is too industrial to be of any real interest to visitors.

If you do decide to go, the best time to visit is during its annual **Fête Interceltique** (inter-Celtic music festival) in early August. Every year thousands of artists descend on the town for the biggest Celtic music event in Brittany. It's advisable to book up well in advance.

In 1666 Lorient took over as the base for the famous French East India Company, formed to promote business with Asia (hence its name, derived from the French for 'the East', *l'Orient*). On the opposite bank of the Blavet river, **Port Louis** is a fairly quiet fishing port and small resort (it was simply called Blavet before the reign of Louis XIII), and has good views over to Lorient. Port Louis also has a small maritime museum, the **Musée de la Compagnie des Indes**, detailing the exploits of the East India trading company.

From Port Louis or Lorient you can catch a boat for the 45-minute trip to **Ile de Groix**, a popular island some 8km (5 miles) long and with plenty of sandy beaches. The diversity of wildfowl species in the area also makes the island a good spot for birdwatching.

Little remains of the ancient fortified town of **Hennebont**, 10km (6 miles) inland from Lorient on the banks of the Blavet. All that can be seen are a few stones, the last vestiges of its protective walls, and the restored Porte du Broerec'h alongside the town's 16th-century church of Notre-Dame-de-Paradis with its tall steeple.

Josselin **

Heading further inland, the small medieval town of **Josselin**, clinging to a hillside overlooking the River Oust, was the stronghold of the Rohan family during the Hundred Years' War. Its castle is a quite stunning piece of architecture – the trio of towers soaring to almost 61m (200ft) punctuate the surrounding countryside. The present structure replaces an earlier castle on the same site

---

FLYING HIGH

The **Tête en l'Air Association**, based in Lorient, organizes kite-flying lessons on Fort Bloque beach all year round; tel: 97.64.73.30.

ILE DE GROIX

Boats depart from Lorient to the Ile de Groix, one of Brittany's many offshore islands, which has a seabird nature reserve as well as an ecology museum; for more details tel: 97.86.84.60.

The fortress-castle of Josselin is reflected in the waters of the River Oust.

that was destroyed by the English in the 12th century. The castle's stable houses the **Musée des Poupées**, a doll museum that displays over 500 dolls dating from the 17th and 18th centuries.

The basilica of Notre-Dame-du-Roncier, founded in the 12th century and Flamboyant in style, contains the tombs of former High Constable of France, Olivier de Clisson, and his wife Marguerite de Rohan.

The approach to Josselin by boat on the River Oust simply cannot be bettered. The surrounding countryside is delightful and well worth exploring. It's also worth taking time to look round Josselin's exceptionally pretty houses and its sections of old ramparts, still visible around the centre of the old town.

Malestroit and Rochefort-en-Terre **

The village of **Malestroit**, also on the River Oust, has many beautiful half-timbered houses in its old centre, especially around the place du Bouffray and the rue du Général-de-Gaulle. Its parish church of St-Gilles, which was originally built in the 12th century, was extended in the 16th century after a fire. The town is a good location from which to hire a boat and make a day trip to Josselin.

Malestroit rather pales into insignificance when compared with the picturesque medieval village of **Rochefort-en-Terre**, which manages to be beautiful without ever being precious. Cobbled streets lined with little granite cottages are strung along a ridge, with a medieval castle and 16th-century church as a backdrop. The town takes its name from the Rochefort family, who built a castle here some time in the 14th century to protect the route between Malestroit and La Roche-Bernard.

Rochefort-en-Terre was flattened during a battle in 1488, when Charles VIII beat the Breton forces of Duke François II during the struggles for control over Brittany by the French crown. Look out for some exceptional 16th- and 17th-century houses as you stroll along rue des Douves, rue Haute-Candre or rue de Porche.

The church of **Notre-Dame-de-la-Tronchaye** is another pleasing feature of the town. Built in the 12th

Half-hidden in its romantic wooded valley setting, the Largoët castle ruins (the Towers of Elven) are the last vestiges of a medieval fortress that belonged to Maréchal de Rieux, a former tutor to Duchess Anne of Brittany.

century, with 15th- and 16th-century embellishments, the church has a fascinating interior, with 16th-century stalls, a wrought iron font and a Renaissance altarpiece. The highlight, however, is a much venerated statue of the Virgin, Notre-Dame-de-la-Tronchaye, believed to date from the time of the Norman invasions. It is the subject of an annual pilgrimage on the Sunday following 15 August.

Southeast of Rochefort, the **Parc de Préhistoire** at Malansac is an educational outdoor museum that contains tableaux depicting life in prehistoric times. Life-size models imaginatively recreate such scenes as the discovery of fire, family life and the setting up of a menhir.

There are more cobbled streets in **Questembert** to the south of Rochefort-en-Terre. The town's chief attractions are its chapel of St-Michel and a 16th-century covered wooden market hall, one of the oldest in France. To the southwest of Questembert is a 16th-century chapel, Notre-Dame-des-Vertus, scene of an annual *pardon* in August.

TOURS D'ELVEN

Heading west from Rochefort-en-Terre, all that remains of the original 11 **Towers of Elven** (also known as the Forteresse de Largoët) are its castle keep and majestic round tower. The castle was destroyed by the French troops of Charles VIII in 1488. Remains include a defensive wall, a gatehouse and the entrance to a tunnel that led to the town of Elven, 3km (2 miles) away.

COSTUME MUSEUM

Not far south of Ploërmel, the **Château du Crévy** is home to an impressive collection of costumes dating from the 18th century to present-day fashions. Period reconstructions illustrate the contemporary tastes of local people from the *ancien régime* to Belle Epoque.

Ploërmel benefits from its location near the forest of Paimpont, and there are plenty of opportunities for walks through established oak and beech trees.

PLOERMEL AND THE NORTHEAST ★★

Ploërmel is a good base for visiting Josselin and the surrounding region of inland Brittany. The town is quite large, though most visitors head straight for its lake, **Etang au Duc**, north of the town. At 2.6 km^2 (1 sq mile), this is Brittany's largest lake and is popular for fishing and watersports. Because of its location near the Forêt de Paimpont (the ancient forest of Brocéliande – see page 46) in the neighbouring department of Ille-et-Vilaine, the land around Ploërmel offers many opportunities for relaxing walks through beautiful countryside.

Ploërmel, originally Plou Artmel, was founded in the 6th century by an Irish missionary. The town later became a seat for the Dukes of Brittany. As a result, it played a major role in military history and was besieged several times by English and French forces between the 12th and 16th centuries. It also suffered badly from bombing in World War II. Today, the only battles that exist are between rival retailers, as the town is a busy shopping and commercial centre. Located to the southeast of Ploërmel, some 700 megaliths at **Monteneuf** make this one of the largest Stone Age sites in Brittany.

Located in the top northeastern corner of Morbihan at the border with Ille-et-Vilaine is the village of **Concoret**. It is near the village of Paimpont, and has tremendous views over the Val des Fées (Valley of the Fairies). Close by at **Comper**, a stately château is reflected in the still waters of the large lake – where, according to legend, Sir Lancelot grew up and from where he took his title 'du Lac'. The medieval fortress is also believed to be the birthplace of the fairy Viviane (Lady of the Lake), who gave the famous sword *Excalibur* to King Arthur (see also page 48).

La Roche-Bernard ★★

Situated on a gorge on the southern extremity of Morbihan, on the edge of the Parc Régional de la Grande Brière, the town of **La Roche-Bernard** is located below a suspension bridge, which replaced a bridge that was accidentally blown up by the Germans in World War II. The remains of the original can still be seen. Amid the town's attractive half-timbered houses is a folk museum containing a collection of rustic and maritime memorabilia. The museum is located in the 17th-century **Château des Basses-Fosses**, formerly a house belonging to a rich merchant. Watersports facilities around here include a canoe and kayak centre, and the town is also a magnet for pleasure boats. La Roche-Bernard is a good place to take a trip on the inland waterway that reaches Dinan and the Rance estuary.

Pontivy and Le Faouët ★★

Right at the heart of inland Brittany lies **Pontivy**, a town famous for its moated castle and beautiful riverside setting. It is a superb base for exploring the lower part of the picturesque Blavet Valley. Near the castle in the town's old quarter are many well-preserved manors and farmhouses. The former workshops that line the rue de Fil are especially worth examining.

Le Faouët in the Ellé Valley, near the border with Finistère, makes for another good inland base and is excellent walking territory, with clearly marked paths

LADY OF THE LAKE

According to legend Lake Comper is where Viviane, daughter of Lord Dymas, brought up the young Lancelot. When he left Viviane to join the court of King Arthur, she captured the magician Merlin and imprisoned him inside 'nine magic circles', where he remained for the rest of his life.

GRISLY REMAINS

In Le Faouët's ossuary look out for the skull of Louis Le Ravallec, who was murdered in 1732 as he returned from a *pardon* at the nearby village of St-Fiacre.

QUIBERON PENINSULA

This popular holiday destination is well known for its
wide range of holiday activities, including water-skiing,
horse-riding, sea-fishing and
sailing. The town of Quiberon
itself is one of Morbihan's
most popular resorts.

ERDEVEN

The resort of Erdeven, which
is located near the top of the
Quiberon peninsula, boasts
an 8km (5-mile) sandy beach
at **Kerhilio**. Like Carnac, it
also has fields of megaliths
among its pine trees and
golden gorse. For further
information, contact the
Syndicat d'Initiative
d'Erdeven, 7 rue Abbé le
Barh, Erdeven, tel:
97.55.64.60.

that wend their way through Ste-Barbe forest. In the
town the Flamboyant Gothic chapel of Ste-Barbe dates
from the 15th century, and is beautifully situated on a
ridge of rocky granite high above a deep ravine gorge,
through which the River Ellé flows. Another Gothic
chapel in the town – the 15th-century St-Fiacre – features
some interesting twisted figures and stained glass detailing the lives of St Fiacre, Christ and brave sailors battling
against a storm. There is also a 16th-century covered
market. To the east, towards Pontivy, a visit to the chapel
in the small village of **Kernascléden** can be a horrifying
experience – images of hell and souls in torment suffering a variety of tortures are depicted in its 15th-century
danse macabre frescoes. You have been warned.

Quiberon **

Quiberon lies at the end of a long spit of land, and in
places the land is not much wider than the road itself.
This is the narrow peninsula (*presqu'île*) of Quiberon. Its
wild and rugged Atlantic shore forms the aptly named
Côte Sauvage, where the waters froth and foam, and the
gorse bushes are twisted into a variety of shapes by the
force of the wind. In Quiberon itself, a former fishing village and now a lively resort, you'll see the inevitable thalassotherapy centres, where visitors pay for the privilege
of being showered, pummelled, massaged and immersed
in fresh seawater for a couple of hours every day.

*Dramatic coastal scenery
along the Côte Sauvage, on
the Quiberon peninsula.*

Quiberon's eastern port is
Port Haliguen, a thriving
yacht harbour with a modern
sheltered marina. There's an
excellent view across to Belle-
Ile as well as the other offshore
islands of **Houat** and **Hoëdic**.
Trips across to the islands
leave from Quiberon's other
harbour, **Port Maria**, which
has a good selection of hotels
and restaurants specializing
in sumptuous fish dishes.

Belle-Ile ★★★

Mention that you're going to **Belle-Ile** and Breton eyes seem to mist over. It is the largest of all Brittany's offshore islands, and, with its high cliffs, small, well-protected creeks and flowered pastures, for many the most romantic.

In high season, between six and eight ferries leave each day for Belle-Ile from Quiberon's Port Maria, and between October and late March ferries depart four to six times a day. Crossings from Quiberon take 45 minutes.

A sign welcomes arrivals to Belle-Ile, only three-quarters of an hour by boat from Quiberon.

Belle-Ile caters mostly for day trippers, and a good way to see the island is by hiring a bike from its port, **Le Palais**, itself a lively town with an interesting historical museum. For children itching to build sandcastles, there is a long, sandy beach–Plage des Grands Sables–between Le Palais and the Kerdonis lighthouse. The island's remoteness has made it a fashionable summer retreat, and it has in the past attracted such luminaries as artist Claude Monet and actress Sarah Bernhardt, who ended up living here. The fort where she resided is now the clubhouse of the island's golf course. Should you, too, wish to remain longer than a day, the island has a

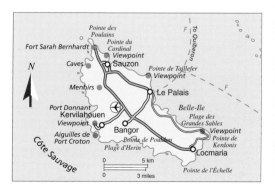

> **ISLAND MAGIC**
>
> According to legend, the Golfe de Morbihan was formed after fairies were chased south out of the forest of Brocéliande. They wept so much that their salty tears created a vast expanse of water, into which they cast their flowered crowns. The petals drifted off to form the estimated 365 islands that are scattered all over the Gulf, while three of the crowns floated out to the ocean – two created the offshore islands of Houat and Hoëdic, but the crown belonging to the fairy queen was transformed into the island of Belle-Ile.

number of hotels and campsites, and there are also some
good fish restaurants.

The fishing port of **Sauzon** on the eastern side of the
island is dramatically situated among sandy cliffs and
coves. There are some fine rock formations at **Pointe des
Poulains**, and an excellent beach at Grandes Sables.

Carnac ★★★

Back on the mainland, the alignments at **Carnac**, where
thousands of mysterious megaliths have stood to attention for over 5000 years, give Morbihan a primitive air.

The huge boulders are set in the ground like mon-
strous headstones, stretching out over fields for a couple
of miles on end. Carnac's three main sites are located just
outside the town. **Kermario** has a dolmen and over 1000
menhirs, including one shaped like a fist. More stones
can be seen at **Kerlescan**, but the largest group is at **Le
Ménec**, numbering nearly 1100 menhirs, with 70 forming
a cromlech, or stone circle.

Just north of the town is the **St-Michel tumulus**. This
is a vast mound of earth and stones covering two burial
chambers and several stone chests. Archaeological exca-
vations have been carried out here, and the artefacts discovered are now on view in Carnac's **Musée de
Préhistoire** (prehistory museum). Alignments of stones
at **Kerzerho** nearby number more than 1100 over a distance of 2km (1¼ miles). The Musée de Préhistoire on
place de la Chapelle, just beyond the site of the stones,
tries to make sense of them all. It has 6000 exhibits from
the Palaeolithic period through the Iron Age and Roman
era to the Middle Ages, and offers a few theories as to
how they got there. At the main menhir field, an *archéo-
scope* promises to take you back in time.

Much religious significance has been attached to the
stones. Some believe Carnac was the Vatican City of prehistoric times, and later clergy attempted to convert the
stones to Christianity simply by daubing a cross on them.
However, like tax returns, it seems Brittany's prehistoric
standing stones weren't meant to be understood. For once
historians know no more than day trippers and no one

The monumental megaliths at Carnac are spread out like a ring of giant's teeth over three main sites – there are over 3000 of the stones in the Carnac district alone. Replanting programmes have attempted to prevent further soil erosion around the alignements *caused by the tread of countless visitors' feet.*

really knows how they got here. Primitive posts for the first fishermen to dry their nets on? A prehistoric cycling proficiency course? Dozens of theories – some more fanciful than others – have been aired over the years as to why the megaliths came to be lined up here at Carnac.

Prehistorians believe the stones may have been astronomical monuments, calendars or places of worship. Others have suggested the stones represented a Stone Age social pecking order, with the most powerful tribes grouped together behind the tallest stones. Engravings on some of the stones suggest fertility worship. Other authorities believe the stones are phallic symbols and that infertile women can cure themselves simply by coating the stones in honey and rubbing their naked bodies against them.

If you want to forget the stones, just west of **La-Trinité-sur-Mer**, a small port with a marina that looks like an upmarket yacht convention, **Carnac-Plage** has a thalassotherapy centre and yacht club as well as dunes and pine woods, evoking childhood memories of first holidays. Its 3km (2 miles) of sandy beaches are becoming increasingly popular with holiday makers.

BULL BY THE HORNS

The 17th-century church in Carnac town is dedicated to St Cornély, patron saint of horned cattle. His statue, flanked on either side by a pair of oxen, can be seen on the church's façade. The custom of bringing diseased cattle to Carnac to be cured is thought to date from Roman times. An annual *pardon* is held in September in honour of the saint.

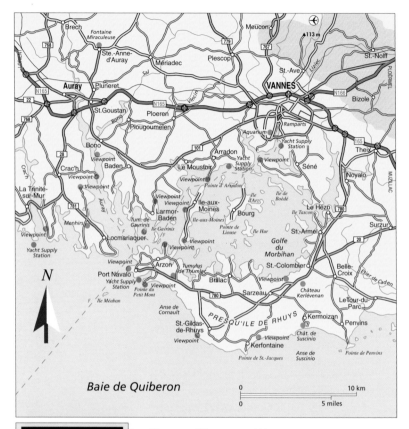

Baie de Quiberon

0   10 km

0   5 miles

GULF TRIPS

Boat tours leave from the Quai de Pen-Lannic, Larmor-Baden; tours are operated by **Les Vedettes Blanches Armor**, tel: 97.57.15.27. Tours also visit the Cairn de Gavrinis all year round.

In the summer **Vedettes du Golfe** operate boat tours of the Gulf; from Apr to Aug they also run tours to Belle-Ile, Houat and Hoëdic.

GOLFE DE MORBIHAN ***

No matter who you ask, you'll always get a different figure for the number of islands in the Golfe de Morbihan. Legend maintains that there are 365 – one for every day of the year – while others claim the number is much lower, arguing that islets that are submerged at high tide do not count as islands. The largest two islands are the tranquil, wooded **Ile des Moines**, a relaxing seaside resort, and the **Ile d'Arz**, with its many megaliths. Several tours of the Gulf are in operation during the summer.

Gavrinis is the island location for one of Morbihan's largest and most spectacular single megaliths, 6m (20ft) high and reached from **Larmor-Baden** via a 15-minute boat crossing. Despite its name, there's nothing German about Larmor-Baden, famed for its oyster beds and its fishing village. **Le Bono** is an ancient oyster port south of Auray, where the River Bono joins the Golfe de Morbihan. It has a picturesque little harbour full of fishing boats, and is an enticing place to stop for a picnic.

Auray ★★

The town of **Auray** is fine for sailing and cruising, and an excellent base if you're planning to stay a while in Morbihan. It has an important place in Breton history books, as it was the site where Jean de Montfort defeated Charles de Blois during the battles for succession to the Duchy of Brittany in 1364.

Better than Auray itself is its port, the delightful old quarter of **St-Goustan**, 2km (1¹/₄ miles) from Auray station. Its medieval stone bridge crosses the Auray river, which bends around steep cobbled streets and half-timbered houses that once belonged to 15th-century shipmasters. St-Goustan's quay is named after the American diplomat and statesman Benjamin Franklin, who landed here in December 1776 en route to negotiate a peace agreement between the French and English during the American war of independence. This area is popular with young people, but has a seedy reputation at night.

LAST OF THE CHOUANS

On Kerléano hill, a small round building topped with a dome marks the tomb of Georges Cadoudal, who was born in Auray in 1771. After the failure of his plot to kidnap Napoleon in Paris, Cadoudal was arrested, sentenced to death and executed in 1804. His remains were brought to his native town and laid to rest on this site, near his family home.

Colourful boats nestle in Auray's harbour in the picturesque St-Goustan quarter. There is an excellent view over the port from the Promenade du Loch.

AURAY

The **Goëlette Musée Saint-Sauveur** (open Apr–Sep) is located on Quai Martin, Vieux Port de St-Goustan, 56400 Auray, tel: 97.56.63.38.

Moored in St-Goustan is the topsail schooner, *Saint-Sauveur*, a reconstructed coastal trader that used to transport pit props to ports in Wales, and then bring back coal to Brittany. Today the schooner (*goëlette*) is a museum, and exhibits include old tools of the shipwright's trade and memorabilia of Auray in bygone days.

Locmariaquer and Ste-Anne-d'Auray ★★

The pretty port of **Locmariaquer** is lined with cottages selling their own oysters, mussels and other shellfish. Its massive megalith – the **Table des Marchands** – lies just off the road. Now broken into slabs, some of which are carved with crook motifs, it once towered 30m (98ft) high. The road ends at the **Pointe de Kerpenhir**, the site of a disused World War II German gun emplacement. There's a fine view of the coast from here.

Ste-Anne-d'Auray is the setting for one of Brittany's most celebrated *pardons* on 25 and 26 July each year. A 19th-century basilica dominates the town, built on the site where, in the early 17th century, an illiterate peasant is said to have discovered a statue of Saint Anne that had lain buried for over nine centuries. Its adjacent convent with medieval cloisters and massive World War I wall memorial is worth a visit, though there is little else to see in this rather sombre pilgrimage town.

The immense Table des Marchands dolmen in the port of Locmariaquer is yet another of Brittany's unexplained megalithic mysteries. The origin of its name – Merchants' Table – has not been satisfactorily resolved.

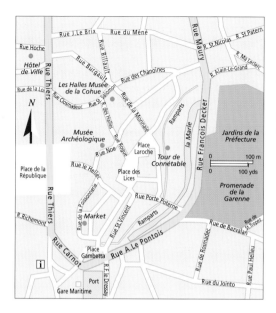

Vannes ★★

The departmental capital of Vannes is an old town of ramparts, ancient squares and top-heavy, half-timbered houses situated 16km (10 miles) east of Auray. At the head of the Golfe de Morbihan, Vannes is surrounded by inlets and creeks, and its attractive old centre of pedestrianized narrow streets offers plenty of visual appeal. Outside the ramparts, however, the urban sprawl of modern Vannes is hardly inspirational.

Within the walled town stands the **Cathédrale de St-Pierre**, 600 years in the making and ranging in architectural styles from Renaissance to Romanesque. The cathedral contains the tomb and relics of Vannes' patron, the Spanish Dominican monk St Vincent, who was famous for his miracle cures and who died here in 1419.

The cathedral has an unusual rotunda chapel, built in the 1530s in an Italian Renaissance style rarely seen in Brittany. The cathedral treasure, housed in the old chapterhouse, includes a 12th-century chest adorned with painted motifs, an ivory cross and several holy vessels.

Vannes' ramparts enclose the old city and overlook some ancient half-timbered wash-houses.

The **Tour de Connétable** (Constable's Tower), named after Bertrand du Guesclin's successor as High Constable of France, Olivier de Clisson, is surrounded by hedges and brightly coloured flowerbeds. Vannes was once capital of the Gallo-Roman empire, and later became home to the Dukes of Brittany. The **Musée Archéologique**, housed in the Château Gaillard, a 15th-century mansion and former parliament building, contains some important prehistoric artefacts, including finds from Carnac.

Vannes' **Port de Plaisance** harbour, gateway to the Golfe de Morbihan and the Atlantic, is now overrun with pleasure craft rather than oyster boats. But a canal leads from the estuary into the heart of old Vannes.

Europe's biggest aquarium, **La Ferme des Marais** (open daily 09:00–11:00, June to August) contains over 600 species of Atlantic and tropical fish in pools that recreate the relevant aquatic environment. Look out for an oyster museum in Vannes' efficient tourist office, itself located in a 16th-century medieval building.

VANNES ARCHITECTURE

One of the most interesting forms of architecture in Vannes are the timber-framed wash-houses (pictured above) beside the River Marle, which runs along the foot of the ramparts.

For a real flavour of what Vannes must have looked like in the Middle Ages, stroll round **place Henri-IV**, edged with well-preserved 16th-century houses with steeply pitched roofs, overhanging gables and tiny windows. More of Vannes' old town houses can be seen in rue St-Salomon and rue des Halles, where you'll also find an entrance to **La Cohue**. These medieval market halls date back to the 13th century, but were later modified, particularly in the 17th century, and were used for fairs until the early 19th century. The building has been sensitively restored and now houses two museums – the **Musée des Beaux-Arts** (fine arts) and the **Musée du Golfe et de la Mer**, with displays on the Gulf's history. It is also an arena for temporary exhibitions.

There is much of architectural interest to engage the attention in Vannes.

Vannes' medieval past is also evoked in the **place des Lices**, a former tournament yard where jousts were staged in 1532, the year of Brittany's union with France. Just over a century earlier, St Vincent was preaching his sermons here, and you can see a statue of the saint ensconced in the niche of a turreted house at one end of the square. The house where St Vincent died is situated at place Valencia, number 17; it remains a splendid example of a timber-framed house with a ground floor in stone.

Leisure activities in Vannes principally centre on watersports, but the city is equally delightful for those intent on less energetic pursuits. The former ducal château, rebuilt in the 19th century and now housing the Law School, has attractive formal flower gardens and a park arranged as a public promenade in the 17th century. The **Promenade de la Garenne** offers fine views of the ramparts and over the city.

VANNES EXCURSION

East of Vannes on the road towards Nantes, the **Château du Plessis-Josso** is situated in a particularly attractive lakeside setting. The castle is composed of three separate parts, from 14th-century manor house to Louis XIII-style pavilion. A visit of the interior takes you through the kitchen, where a formidable granite stove with holes for heating platters is on display.

Right: *View of the former abbey church, St-Gildas-de-Rhuys. A monastery was founded here in the 6th century by St Gildas; among the most famous of its abbots was Peter Abélard, who governed here in the 12th century. Abélard found life difficult in what he called 'a wild country', inhabited by a people whose language he considered 'strange and horrible'.*

Opposite: *Le Croisic is an important centre for the cultivation of shellfish. Fishing boats and pleasure craft dock side by side in its harbour.*

SUSCINIO

In a wild, windswept setting on the coast, its moat originally filled by the sea, the castle of Suscinio is an impressive medieval fortress. The castle was confiscated by the French crown after Brittany's union with France, and it suffered severe damage during the Revolution. The museum inside the entrance buildings illustrates the history of Brittany through portraits, paintings and some exquisitely produced local artefacts, including fine 14th-century ceramic floor coverings.

RHUYS PENINSULA **

Just north of **Sarzeau**, a small town with a 16th-century church and square with Renaissance houses, is the 14th-century **Château de Suscinio**. Its large ramparts and six defensive towers still make an imposing sight. Now housing a museum, the castle was formerly a summer residence of the Dukes of Brittany.

St-Gildas-de-Rhuys has menhirs standing in a blackberry field. Nearby is a hill called Caesar's Mound, where the Roman leader reputedly stood and watched his last Gallic enemies, the Veneti, defeated at sea in 56BC. There is good sailing from the long beaches all along the Rhuys Peninsula.

As you head south from the Rhuys Peninsula towards the Parc Naturel Régional de la Grande Brière, technically you leave the department of Morbihan – and Brittany itself – once you've crossed the River Vilaine and enter the Loire-Atlantique.

La Baule **

At the popular beach resort of **La Baule**, it's as though a slice of the Mediterranean has been deposited in Brittany. The resort has smart shops and 9km (5¹/₂ miles) of south-facing golden sands. Billed as the most beautiful beach in Brittany, La Baule has spawned a multitude of slogans such as 'the Nice of the North'. Beware: in the summer, it can be incredibly packed, and hotels and restaurants operate only two prices – expensive and very expensive. The designer sunglasses of the nearly famous now head to the chic resort that stretches between the suburb **Pornichet** to La Baule.

At nearby **Batz-sur-Mer**, the rocky coastline is punctuated by the sandy beaches of Port-Lin and Valentin, which are quieter and very good for swimming. **Le Croisic** is a good spot for freshly caught crab, lobster and bass when in season. It also has a naval museum and an aquarium, and is a popular location for skin-diving.

PARC DES DRYADES

Situated near the place des Palmiers in La Baule-les-Pins, this beautifully landscaped park with its many varieties of trees and ornamental flower beds provides a welcome green retreat from the rigours of the beach.

THE LOIRE ESTUARY

West of La Baule, **Guérande** will come as a breath of fresh air after all that sand. This is a medieval market town with its 15th-century ramparts still intact. Its four fortified gateways used to guard the salt pans of Guérande, for which the town is famous. A museum in one of the gatehouses explains the history of the town's salt industry, and has interesting displays of artefacts.

St-Nazaire was an important German submarine base during World War II and was virtually destroyed. A post-war rebuilding programme seemed to put the emphasis firmly on concrete.

This shipbuilding town has two major claims to fame. Its **Pont de St-Nazaire-St-Brévin**, which rises majestically over the Loire estuary, is the longest road bridge in France. Its other claim concerns heavy loss of life. At the end of March 1942, a British destroyer packed full of explosives rammed the gates of St-Nazaire and put it out of action. However, the Allies paid a high price, losing two-thirds of their commandos, and German soldiers took reprisals against local people. A commemorative column beside the harbour lists the dead.

What it lacks in architectural charm, St-Nazaire makes up for in sporting facilities, especially in the **Parc Paysager**, which has a swimming pool, a lake, tennis courts and picnic areas.

On the western outskirts of St-Nazaire lies **St-Marc-sur-Mer**, an archetypal seaside resort of Southern Brittany, where Jacques Tati filmed his famous *Monsieur Hulot's Holiday* in the 1950s. Just inland are the marshlands of **La Grande Brière**, a huge nature preserve that provides a striking contrast to the surrounding fleshpots.

The Grande Brière park covers an area of 40,000ha (96,160 acres), at the centre of which is an extensive marsh that is freely accessible to visitors. Boat trips along bullrush-fringed channels are one of the best ways to see the park, offering glimpses of an almost vanished pastoral landscape. There is also a path that runs through the park, with observation posts and descriptive panels to help you identify the surrounding flora and fauna.

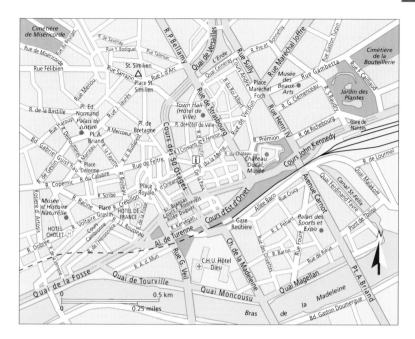

Nantes ★★

Nantes is no longer officially part of Brittany, but it cannot be separated either spiritually or historically. Elected as the Breton capital in the 10th century, Nantes continued to hold this honour until the 1960s, when the modern administrative region of Pays de la Loire was established in a move that also deprived Brittany of St-Nazaire and the prime resort of La Baule.

A port at the head of the Loire estuary, today Nantes is a large modern city. Like Brest and Lorient, Nantes was almost destroyed beyond recognition by World War II bombardments. It was here, too, that the anti-Nazi French Resistance movement was started.

The city is named after the Gallic tribe of the Namnetes, whose main settlement it was before the tribe was conquered by Julius Caesar. Between the 16th and 19th centuries, Nantes' middle classes grew rich from the city's location at the centre of France's African slave trade.

BRETON CAPITAL

First Gallic and then Roman, Nantes was heavily involved in the struggles for control of the region between Frankish kings and Breton noblemen. In 843, Viking pirates landed and invaded the cathedral, putting the Bishop and the entire congregation to death. It wasn't until 939, when Alain Barbe-Torte returned from England, that the invaders were driven out of Brittany once and for all. As duke, Alain Barbe-Torte chose Nantes for his capital and set about rebuilding it. Nantes was also capital of the Duchy of Brittany in the Middle Ages.

The high-vaulted nave and five carefully decorated arched entrances of Nantes' **Cathédrale de St-Pierre et St-Paul** still survive. The cathedral was badly damaged during liberation in 1944, and a severe fire swept through it in 1972, but it has since mercifully been restored. The cathedral contains the tombs of Duke François II and his wife Marguerite, parents of Duchess Anne.

Château des Ducs de Bretagne

The **Château des Ducs de Bretagne** at place Marc Elder is definitely worth visiting. Begun in the mid-15th century, this was the ducal residence of the last two independent rulers of Brittany, François II and his daughter, Duchess Anne, who was born here in 1477. It was on Anne's orders that the horseshoe-shaped **Tour du Fer à Cheval** and the **Tour de la Couronne d'Or** were built.

The château lays claim to two other notable events in French and Breton history: it was here that the alleged satanist, Gilles de Rais, whose activities are said to have spawned the legend of Bluebeard, was tried and publicly executed in 1440; and here, too, Henri IV signed the Edict of Nantes in 1598 (subsequently revoked in 1685 by Louis XIV) that brought to an end the Wars of Religion between Catholics and Protestants.

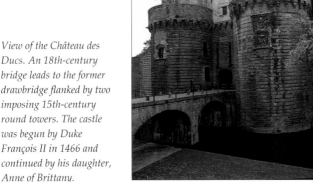

View of the Château des Ducs. An 18th-century bridge leads to the former drawbridge flanked by two imposing 15th-century round towers. The castle was begun by Duke François II in 1466 and continued by his daughter, Anne of Brittany.

Nantes Museums

Nantes has many interesting museums, and two of the best are located in the Château des Ducs de Bretagne. The first is the **Musée d'Art Populaire Régional**, which features collections of peasant costume, traditional furniture and household wares.

The **Musée des Salorges** tells the story of Nantes' famous triangular trade. Ships armed with French manufactured goods would set sail to the west coast of Africa; here they would take on board Africans destined to be sold into the slave trade in plantations in the West Indies. The ships then returned to Nantes loaded with sugar cane to swell its refineries. The trade in black slaves financed much building work in the city, for example the Place Graslin, the Ile Feydeau (the smart commercial district) and construction of its docks.

The heart of Duchess Anne of Brittany is said to be kept in the **Musée Dobrée** in place Jean V, along with other things essentially Breton, including tapestries, ceramics and furnishings. The building, a Romanesque-style house erected in the 19th century, belonged to the Nantes ship-owner and art collector Thomas Dobrée.

Never mind the museums, there's plenty of outdoor activity in this lively cosmopolitan city.

OTHER MUSEUMS IN NANTES

The **Musée Jules Verne** (3 rue de l'Hermitage) honours Nantes' best known author, responsible for *Around the World in Eighty Days* and *Twenty Thousand Leagues Under the Sea*.

In the Quai de la Fosse, there is a disused navy destroyer, the *Maillé-Brézé*, which is now a **floating naval museum**. It is full of anti-aircraft weaponry – fortunately all since made safe. Open in summer months daily. Closed Mon.

Morbihan and Nantes at a Glance

BEST TIMES TO VISIT

Morbihan enjoys a settled climate year-round; if you're not looking to spend your time frying on the beach, a visit outside the busy summer months can be advantageous. It's sensible to book well in advance if you do intend to stay in popular resorts such as Belle-Ile, La Baule and other seaside destinations on the Golfe de Morbihan, or if you plan to visit Lorient during the inter-Celtic music festival in August. Bear in mind, also, that many hotels and restaurants close for the winter.

GETTING THERE

Brit Air (tel: 0181-742 6600) and Air France operate regular **flights** from London-Gatwick to Nantes.

GETTING AROUND

TTO Buses travel from Vannes to Rennes via Josselin; to Nantes via La Roche-Bernard; to Quiberon via Auray and other destinations; tel: 97.47.29.64.

There is a regular **train** service (five times daily) between Redon, Quimper and Brest, stopping at Questembert, Vannes and Auray.

Ferries to Belle-Ile from Quiberon take 45 min; there are 10 per day between July and September, and between two and four crossings a day the rest of the year; for the latest information, tel: 97.31.80.01.

In Nantes, **bicycles** can be hired from Séguir Bernard, 38 rue des Alouettes, tel: 40.46.56.32. Bicycles are also available for hire from the SNCF (railway station) at Nantes; tel: 40.08.50.50.

WHERE TO STAY

Ploërmel
Hôtel Le Cobh, 10 rue des Forges, charming Logis de France hotel that also has an excellent restaurant, with an award-winning chef; in the restaurant, look out for a horse saddle and a large primitive bottle opener, tel: 97.74.00.49.

Carnac
Les Alignements, 45 rue St-Cornély, aptly named and reasonably priced hotel, tel: 97.52.06.30.

Auray
Hôtel Le Marin, 1 place du Rolland, St-Goustan, well-priced hotel in 300-year-old building that used to belong to the Breton navy (*Royale*); the hotel, conveniently situated in the medieval port of St-Goustan, is run by a man with probably the largest moustache in Brittany, tel: 97.24.14.58.

Locmariaquer
Le Relais de Kerpenhir, pleasant hotel and restaurant open all year and located near the beaches of the Golfe de Morbihan, tel: 97.57.31.20, fax: 97.57.36.35.

Vannes
Vannes offers probably the best selection of hotels in the Golfe de Morbihan, though if you plan to stay during peak season it's as well to book ahead.
Hôtel Mascotte, rue Jean-Monnet, an inexpensive, modern hotel within walking distance of Vannes' medieval centre, tel: 97.47.59.60.
Hôtel La Bretagne, 34–6 rue du Méné, pleasant, well-placed hotel – some rooms have good views of the ramparts, tel: 97.47.20.21.

La Baule
Hôtel Ty Gwenn, 24 avenue Grande Dune, good value for money, located near the beach at La Baule-les-Pins, no restaurant, tel: 40.60.37.07.

Nantes
Nantes has a phenomenal number of hotels to choose from – well over 100 registered establishments within the city. There's something to meet almost every budget.

Caravanners and campers are also well provided for – there is an efficiently managed municipal camping site, the **Val du Cens**, some 3km (2 miles) north of the city centre in boulevard du Petit-Port.

For budget travellers, Nantes has three youth hostels, two of which are open year-round. The summer-only hostel is in a former tobacco factory at place de la Manu,

Morbihan and Nantes at a Glance

off boulevard Stalingrad.

WHERE TO EAT

Auray
L'Eglantine, 17 place St-Sauveur, St-Goustan, it is advisable to book as the restaurant can be very busy; specializes in fish and traditional cuisine; closed Wednesdays, tel: 97.56.46.55.

Vannes
Régis Mahé, place Gare, a bit out of the way, but serves superb *bouillon de sole et coquillages*, tel: 97.42.61.41.
La Marée Bleue, 8 place Bir-Hakeim, seafood and traditional Breton cuisine, closed Sunday evenings, tel: 97.47.24.29.

La Baule
La Cigale, 4 place Graslin, well-located restaurant specializing in fish, overlooks the ocean, tel: 40.61.76.41.

Nantes
Le Chiwawa, 6 place Eugène Livet, good seafood *à la nouvelle cuisine*, very popular, and serves generous portions, tel: 40.69.01.65.
Le Colvert, 14 rue Armand Brossard, reasonable restaurant that serves excellent Breton dishes *au beurre blanc*, tel: 40.48.20.02.

TOURS AND EXCURSIONS

Branféré Wildlife Park: animal sanctuary set in botanic gardens of a château, located at Le Guerno between Vannes

and La Roche-Bernard. Open daily all year round; tel: 97.42.94.66, fax: 97.42.81.22.
Boat trips around the Golfe de Morbihan: a circular trip around the islands of the Gulf starts from Locmariaquer. Several departures during the day from Locmariaquer between 09:00 and 19:00 in season. Operated by **Les Vedettes**, tel: 97.57.30.29.
Musée de la Compagnie des Indes, Port Louis: the museum traces the maritime history of the Morbihan-based Indies Companies that created trade relations with Africa, India and China during the 17th and 18th centuries; tel: 97.82.19.13.
Citadelle Vauban de Belle-Ile: military architect Vauban's Belle-Ile citadel towers over Le Palais harbour. A museum explains the island's military and maritime history. Open every day all year 09:30–19:00; tel: 97.31.84.17.
Musée des Poupées, 3 rue des Trentes, Josselin: located in the former stables of Josselin castle is the Rohan collection of family dolls, started in 1880 by the great-

grandmother of the present owners; tel: 97.22.36.45.
Brittany Prehistoric Gardens: just northeast of Questembert at Malansac. In an outside setting displays range from dinosaurs measuring 15m (49ft) tall to Brittany's first human inhabitants in the Neolithic era; tel: 97.43.34.17.
Alfred's Museum: in Nivillac, near La Roche-Bernard, the museum features a wide variety of old objects or antiques – anything from old toys to cars, motorcycles and bicycles make up the memorabilia. Open all year 10:00–12:00 and 14:00–19:00.

USEFUL CONTACTS

Office du Tourisme du Pays de Vannes, 1 rue Thiers, tel: 97.47.24.34, fax: 97.47.29.49.
Office du Tourisme de Belle-Ile en Mer, tel: 97.31.81.93, fax: 97.31.56.17.
Office du Tourisme de Nantes, place Aristide-Briand, tel: 40.61.03.88.
Syndicat d'Initiative de l'Île de Groix, tel: 97.05.53.08.
Syndicat d'Initiative de La Baule, 8 place Victoire, tel: 40.24.34.44.

NANTES	J	F	M	A	M	J	J	A	S	O	N	D
AVERAGE TEMP. °F	40	40	46	50	58	64	68	68	64	56	48	42
AVERAGE TEMP. °C	5	5	8	10	14	17	19	19	17	13	9	6
Hours of Sun Daily	2	3	5	6	7	8	9	8	6	5	3	2
RAINFALL in	3	3	3	2	3	2	2	2	2	3	3	3
RAINFALL mm	87	70	70	50	64	45	46	45	62	79	87	84
Days of Rainfall	17	15	15	14	16	11	10	11	12	14	16	16

Travel Tips

Best Times to Visit

The best weather for a seaside holiday is normally late June and July, as the crowds do not usually arrive until August. Brittany is one of France's preferred holiday destinations, so if you're going during July and August, reservations are essential.

Most hotels open their doors to tourists only from June to mid-September, but if you're going in winter, a surprising number of hotels and restaurants are open all year round.

If you go out of season, you won't have the crowds to contend with; on the other hand, you won't have the weather on your side, either. You'll also see the signs *fermé* and *fermeture annuelle* – annual closure – with alarming regularity. If you want to make an evening of it, don't leave going out to dinner too late, as establishments tend to close early – sometimes as early as 21:30.

Tourist Information

Tourist information offices in Brittany come under two different names. They will generally be called *Office du Tourisme*, but in smaller towns look out for the sign *Syndicat d'Initiative* (SI). Both can give suggestions for places to visit and give advice on travel arrangements. Some excellent maps are available, although in some places a small fee may be charged.

Entry Documents

Citizens of European Union countries, Japan, Canada and the United States who hold a valid passport do not need a visa for stays of less than three months. Visitors from other countries, including Australia, New Zealand and South Africa, will need to apply for a visa from their nearest French consulate before entry into France.

Getting to Brittany

By ferry: Brittany Ferries operates a daily sailing (in summer only) between Portsmouth and St-Malo (9hr), and between Plymouth and Roscoff (6hr). Off season, there are crossings twice a week. For reservations and further details, contact Brittany Ferries, tel: (01705) 827701.

Via *Le Shuttle*: Since the opening of the Channel Tunnel in 1994 the range of options for travellers to France from the UK has increased. The tunnel emerges well to the east of Brittany, in the Pas de Calais, and its impact on travel to this particular region of France is difficult to assess. It seems likely that ferries will continue to provide the most convenient option for many visitors, although the frequency of services and short transit times offered by *Le Shuttle* will have a distinct appeal. Trains operated by *Le Shuttle* run between Folkestone and Calais every 15 min; journey time is a mere 35 min, and passengers stay with their vehicles for the duration.

By air: Brit Air flies daily from London-Gatwick to Brest, Quimper, Nantes and Rennes; tel: (01293) 502044 for information. It's also worth looking out for flights to Paris, because some stop en route in Brittany.

By train: Since 1989 the *TGV*

Atlantique high-speed train route through Brittany has drastically reduced travelling time from Paris; the journey from the French capital to Rennes or Nantes now takes just 2hr. The *Eurostar* train service between London's Waterloo International and Paris Gare du Nord via the Channel Tunnel takes 3hr.

Getting Around

By road: Brittany enjoys a good network of roads. The speed limit on the tolled motorways (*autoroutes*) is 130kph (80mph); on dual carriageways it is 110kph (68mph), and on other main roads the limit is 90kph (56mph). Remember to slow down when entering towns and villages, as the speed limit reduces to 50kph (30mph).

The French drive on the right, pass on the left. An important rule to remember is that drivers should normally yield to traffic approaching from the right (*priorité à droite*). A yellow diamond-shaped sign with a white border indicates that drivers on main roads have the right of way and do not need to give way to the right. When the sign reappears with a diagonal line through it, then the *priorité à droite* rule again comes into force.

By bike: As you'd expect from a country that hosts the most famous annual cycle race, Brittany is superb cycling country. It's probably no exaggeration to say that France is the most cyclist-friendly place in the world. French motoring

laws dictate that drivers must give cyclists a car's width when overtaking, and attitudes towards cyclists are generally very positive.

Bicycles can be hired from most main railway stations as well as from some tourist offices and bicycle shops. If you take your own bike, it's wise to carry a puncture repair outfit and spare inner tubes with you.

Hitch-hiking: *Faire le stop* is a good way to get around if you're young, fit or on a shoestring budget – or all three. It will be easier to get a lift in summer, but it's unlikely you'll have to wait very long, even off season. Hitch-hiking is also a good way of practising your French. A few basic rules apply: don't hitch-hike on motorways (*autoroutes*), and don't leave it too late in the day; when it gets dark, your chances of getting a lift are dramatically reduced. It's safest to travel in twos. Trust your instincts – if you don't like the look of the driver offering you a lift, don't get in. And finally, smile and try to make conversation. The driver doesn't have to give you a lift, and more often than not he or she is only too keen to help you out.

What Clothes to Pack

More than anything else (even more than children's buckets and spades), you'll need to take a waterproof, wind-resistant coat, no matter what time of year. You're better off bringing a raincoat rather than an umbrella since, if it's

windy as well, you won't be spending all your time trying to remain on the ground.

In summer, when the temperature averages around 20°C (70°F), it's advisable to bring lightweight clothing as well as a jacket to protect against the winds. Beachwear and a good sunfilter are also sensible for holidays on the coast. Be prepared, however, for strong sea breezes which can lower the temperature quite considerably.

Money Matters

You don't need to be an oil tycoon to have an enjoyable stay. Brittany is not that expensive, and it's certainly a lot cheaper than the south of France. The currency is French francs (written as F or FF), and 100 centimes make one franc. Notes come in denominations of 20, 50, 100, 200 and 500FF. Coins come in denominations of 10, 5, 2 and 1FF, and 50, 20, 10 and 5 centimes.

It's worthwhile shopping around to find the best exchange rate. Traveller's cheques and foreign currency can be changed at banks displaying the sign *Change* – remember to take along your passport. Independent *bureaux de change* and many hotels can also change currency, but usually at less favourable rates.

Credit cards are widely accepted as a means of payment, except in some of Brittany's more remote towns and villages. Also accepted are Eurocheques, used with a cheque card and drawn against your bank account, and certain cashpoint cards issued by the main British banks that debit your British current account directly.

Tipping

Hotel and restaurant bills usually include a service charge, but if you feel the service has been particularly special, a tip will be appreciated, perhaps between 10 and 15% of the total bill.

Accommodation

With 1138 hotels, 28,000 hotel rooms, 12,000 self-catering units and 850 camp-sites, all types of accommodation are available in Brittany. Your choice of where to stay obviously depends on a number of factors – budgetary constraints, whether you plan to travel around or stay put, whether accessibility or remoteness is the key consideration, and so on. A certain amount of forward planning is essential if you intend visiting in July and August, when accommodation is especially difficult to find.

Hotels are classified using a star rating by the French Ministry of Tourism, and prices are generally consistent with the number of stars. Ungraded and one-star hotels offer basic accommodation, though they frequently represent good value. Prices are charged per room, and there's a supplement for additional beds or cots; breakfast is usually extra. For some recommendations, consult the 'At a Glance' sections for each chapter.

For those who prefer **self-catering**, Brittany has a huge selection of *gîtes*, ranging from simple converted farm buildings to elegant manor houses. Many may be off the beaten track, so transport is essential. In the UK, private owners frequently advertise holiday rentals in the Sunday newspapers; otherwise, Gîtes de France is the French government service that can arrange bookings in any one of its hundreds of properties; they can be contacted on 0171-493 3480.

Bed-and-breakfast accommodation (*chambres d'hôte*) is sometimes available in country areas and is usually inexpensive, though standards vary. Tourist information offices can supply details.

Campsites are almost everywhere in Brittany, particularly along the coast. They are rated using the star system, as for hotels. The most economical option is the *camping municipal*, which provides facilities such as hot water. Other categories of campsite offering superior facilities, including bars and restaurants, are likely to be popular and advance booking may be a wise precaution.

Electricity

220-volt electricity is generally available in Brittany, though some rural areas may use 110 volts. Two-pin round plugs are widely used in the whole of France, so if you must bring your toaster or hair-dryer, make sure you bring an adaptor, available from most electrical retailers.

Telephones

International and long-distance calls can be made from any phone box in Brittany. To make an international call, dial 19 and wait until there is a continuous burring tone. For a reverse-charge call ask for *un appel en PCV* ('pey, sey, vey').

Health Requirements

It's wise to make sure that your health insurance policy covers you for accident or illness while you're on holiday. Visitors from EU countries

CONVERSION CHART		
FROM	**TO**	**MULTIPLY BY**
Millimetres	inches	0.0394
Metres	yards	1.0936
Metres	feet	3.281
Kilometres	miles	0.6214
Hectares	acres	2.471
Litres	pints	1.760
Kilograms	pounds	2.205
Tonnes	tons	0.984
To convert Celsius to Fahrenheit: x 9 ÷ 5 + 32		

with corresponding health insurance facilities are entitled to medical and hospital treatment under French social security arrangements; you'll need to have the appropriate E111 form, available from your post office. Chemists (*pharmacies*) display a green cross; despite selling fragrant perfumes and aftershaves, they are extremely helpful if you're in need of medical assistance.

Emergencies

Bretons are a kind people and, although they may sometimes appear distant and aloof, are more than ready to render assistance if you're in any kind of trouble. To phone the police, just dial 17; for the fire brigade, dial 18.

Security and Safety

Use your common sense and you should have a trouble-free holiday. All the usual rules apply. Lock your car at all times. Don't bring anything of real value with you, but if you must, make sure you keep it locked in the hotel safe. Keep an eye on your wallet, bag and personal belongings in crowds and tourist areas, as pickpockets and thieves do operate.

In Brittany, however, there is a far greater risk of danger from natural elements than from human ones. In some places the sea is extremely dangerous – it may look tempting, but powerful currents can overwhelm even the strongest swimmer. So, unless a beach is obviously

PUBLIC HOLIDAYS

1 January – New Year's Day
April – Easter Monday
1 May – Labour Day
8 May – Victory Day
May – Ascension
May or June – Whitsun
15 August – Assumption
1 November – All Saints' Day
11 November – Armistice Day
25 December – Christmas Day

intended for bathing, don't attempt a swim without seeking advice first. Look out for the different coloured flags. A green flag means that the beach is fine for swimming; an orange one means that swimming is dangerous, but there is a lifeguard on duty. Beware of the red flag, which means that swimming is forbidden. If you get out of your depth in the waters of these beaches, not even the best travel insurance in the world can help you.

Trading Hours

The weekend tends to start later in Brittany. As Saturday is considered to be more of a working day, many shops are closed on Monday. To avoid disappointment, it's worth remembering that many restaurants are closed on Sunday evenings and all day Monday.

Food shops tend to open early. Larger shops and department stores open from between 09:00 and 10:00. Virtually everything shuts down for lunch from noon until 14:00 or even later, so if you plan on eating a picnic

lunch, make sure you buy your provisions before midday. Most shops close their doors at around 18:30 or 19:00, later in summer in the resort areas.

Time Difference

France is one hour ahead of Greenwich Mean Time. When it is midday in London, it will be 13:00 in Brittany.

Language

Breton is a language, not a dialect, though it's not necessary to speak it. A working knowledge of French will be fine – extremely useful, in fact, especially away from the larger main cities and towns. Of course, you will be able to get away with speaking English, though it will most certainly increase your enjoyment of your holiday if you can converse with the locals. Even the smallest effort to speak French will be appreciated, especially in less touristy areas.

Pardons
25–26 July – Ste-Anne-d'Auray
26 July – Brech, Quistinic
1 August – Pluméliau
2 August – Persquen
15 August – Guern, Plougoumélen, Perros-Guirec, Rostrénen, Pont-Croix
16 August – Carantec, Rochefort-en-Terre, Ploërdut
22–24 August – Le Faouët
30 August – Ste-Anne-la-Palud
6 September – Camors, Camaret, St-Guénolé-Pouldreuzic, Le Folgoët

USEFUL EXPRESSIONS

Introductions

Hello/Good day *Bonjour (Monsieur/Madame)*
Good evening *Bonsoir*
Thank you (very much) *Merci (beaucoup)*
Please *S'il vous plaît*
You're welcome *Je vous en prie*
What's your name? *Comment vous appelez-vous?*
My name is . . . *Je m'appelle . . .*
How are you? *Comment allez-vous?/Ça va?*
Very well, thanks *Très bien, merci*
Goodbye *Au revoir*
See you soon *A bientôt*
See you tomorrow *A demain*
OK *D'accord*
Do you speak English? *Parlez-vous anglais?*
Can you speak slower? *Parlez moins vite, s'il vous plaît.*
I don't understand. *Je ne comprends pas.*
I don't know. *Je ne sais pas.*

Asking questions

How much/How many? *Combien?*
Where? *Où?*
How? *Comment?*
When? *Quand?*
Why? *Pourquoi?*
At what time? *A quelle heure?*
Where is . . .? *Où est . . . ?/ Où se trouve . . . ?*
How far is . . . ? *A quelle distance se trouve . . . ?*
How long does it take to get to . . . ? *Ça prend combien de temps pour aller jusqu'à . . . ?*

Finding Accommodation

Do you have a double room for tonight? *Avez-vous une chambre pour deux personnes pour cette nuit?*
a room with shower/bath/toilet *une chambre avec douche/salle de bain/toilettes*
for one/two/three nights *pour une/deux/trois nuits*
What's the rate per night? *Quel est le prix pour une nuit?*
Is breakfast included? *Est-ce que le petit déjeuner est compris?*
The key, please. *La clef, s'il vous plaît.*
Can we camp here? *On peut camper ici?*
a campsite *un camping/un terrain de camping*
a tent *une tente*
a tent space *un emplacement*

On the Road

Car park *un parking*
No parking *Défense de stationner/stationnement interdit*
Fill the tank up, please. *Le plein, s'il vous plaît.*
lead-free *sans plomb*
petrol *essence*
oil *huile*
My car has broken down. *Ma voiture est en panne.*
The battery's dead. *La batterie est morte.*
insurance *assurance*

Road Signs

Accotements non stabilisés Soft shoulders
Chaussée déformée Uneven road surface
Déviation Detour
Péage Toll
Piste cyclable Cycle path
Priorité à droite Yield to traffic from the right
Ralentir Slow down
Serrez à droite/à gauche Keep right/left

Eating Out

I'd like to reserve a table *Je voudrais réserver une table*
Do you have vegetarian dishes? *Avez-vous des plats végétariens?*
I'll have… *Je prendrai…*
May I have some…? *Pourrais-je avoir…?*
bread *du pain*
butter *du beurre*
black coffee *un café noir*
bread rolls *des petits pains*
coffee with milk *un café au lait*

Snacks

crêpe pancake
crêpe à la confiture pancake with jam
crêpe aux œufs pancake with eggs
croque-monsieur grilled ham and cheese sandwich
œufs brouillés scrambled eggs
œufs durs hard-boiled eggs
œufs au plat fried eggs
omelette nature plain omelette
omelette au fromage cheese omelette

INDEX